NERDS

ALSO BY DAVID ANDEREGG

Worried All the Time: Rediscovering the Joy
in Parenthood in an Age of Anxiety

Jeremy P. Tarcher/Penguin

a member of Penguin Group (USA) Inc.

New York

NERDS

HOW DORKS, DWEEBS, TECHIES, AND TREKKIES CAN SAVE AMERICA AND WHY THEY MIGHT BE OUR LAST HOPE

DAVID ANDEREGG, PH.D.

JEREMY P. TARCHER/PENGUIN
Published by the Penguin Group
Penguin Group (USA) Inc., 375 Hudson Street, New York, New York 10014, USA · Penguin Group
(Canada), 90 Eglinton Avenue East, Suite 700, Toronto, Ontario M4P 2Y3, Canada (a division of
Pearson Penguin Canada Inc.) · Penguin Books Ltd, 80 Strand, London WC2R 0RL, England ·
Penguin Ireland, 25 St Stephen's Green, Dublin 2, Ireland (a division of Penguin Books Ltd) ·
Penguin Group (Australia), 250 Camberwell Road, Camberwell, Victoria 3124, Australia
(a division of Pearson Australia Group Pty Ltd) · Penguin Books India Pvt Ltd, 11 Community Centre,
Panchsheel Park, New Delhi–110 017, India · Penguin Group (NZ), 67 Apollo Drive, Rosedale,
North Shore 0632, New Zealand (a division of Pearson New Zealand Ltd) · Penguin Books
(South Africa) (Pty) Ltd, 24 Sturdee Avenue, Rosebank, Johannesburg 2196, South Africa

Penguin Books Ltd, Registered Offices: 80 Strand, London WC2R 0RL, England

First trade paperback edition 2011

Most Tarcher/Penguin books are available at special quantity discounts for bulk purchase for sales
promotions, premiums, fund-raising, and educational needs. Special books or book excerpts also can
be created to fit specific needs. For details, write Penguin Group (USA) Inc. Special Markets, 375
Hudson Street, New York, NY 10014.

The Library of Congress catalogued the hardcover as follows:

Anderegg, David, date.
Nerds : how dorks, dweebs, techies, and trekkies can save America and
why they might be our last hope / David Anderegg.
p.   cm.
Includes bibliographical references and index.
ISBN 978-1-58542-590-7
1. Gifted children—Social conditions—United States.   2. Children with social disabilities—
United States.   3. Stereotypes (Social psychology)—United States.   4. Prejudices—
United States.   5. Popular culture—United States.   I. Title.
LC3993.9.A84   2007   2007036005
371.95—dc22

ISBN 978-1-58542-852-6 (paperback edition)

Printed in the United States of America

1   3   5   7   9   10   8   6   4   2

BOOK DESIGN BY MEIGHAN CAVANAUGH

Some names and identifying characteristics have been changed to protect the privacy of the individuals involved.

While the author has made every effort to provide accurate telephone numbers and Internet addresses at the time of publication, neither the publisher nor the author assumes any responsibility for errors, or for changes that occur after publication. Further, the publisher does not have any control over and does not assume any responsibility for author or third-party websites or their content.

For Kelley

love, all ways

ACKNOWLEDGMENTS

Where does one start? To begin at the beginning, I would have to thank my old teacher Mrs. Holman, for giving me the part of the Dictionary in our fourth-grade play at the Henry G. Rosenow School in Fond du Lac, Wisconsin. That experience playing a know-it-all, and the play itself, made me ask myself a lot of questions, which I am finally getting around to answering. So thank you, Mrs. Holman . . . I think.

But later-arriving bystanders deserve much more in the way of gratitude. I wish to thank Gareth Esersky and Carol Mann for their persistent belief in this project, and Kat Kimball and Sara Carder at Tarcher/Penguin for their diligent efforts to see it through. Dean Elissa Tenny at Bennington College supported the project early on, and I am grateful for her support.

My students at Bennington, all of them, have been my guides, my cheerleaders, and my windows on the world of popular culture. The students in my research seminar, where we spent an entire year hip-deep in nerds, deserve a special nod: Zach

Hill, Danny Grossman, Spencer Binney, Sera Vautier, and Nina Rudnick—may you all live long and prosper.

Many other informants, of course, have given me the gift of their time and thoughtful answers to my nagging questions. These include my patients and their parents and the other kids I talk to—neighbors, nephews, and total strangers. Thank you, one and all, for thinking out loud and allowing me to listen.

Writer friends always need to be thanked—they get so little gratitude elsewhere. I wish to thank one particularly encouraging writer pal, Michelle Gillett, whose simple question "Are we dweebs?" has been an endless source of inspiration.

My wife, Kelley DeLorenzo, serves as my chief critic and my biggest fan—two unrewarding jobs that are even more unrewarding when performed simultaneously. Thank you, dear Kelley, for your constant love and protection.

CONTENTS

NERDS

INTRODUCTION TO THE PAPERBACK EDITION

When *Nerds* first appeared, at the very end of 2007, I felt I was asking my readers to do a simple task: just look at this one ingrained American prejudice, and look at its effects. That's all. I wasn't asking readers to solve Fermat's Theorem, or to understand once and for all the mysteries of Keynesian economics. I asked people to think about what we tell our children about those people we call "nerds," and think for a minute about what message we might be sending. I know; it seems naive now, but that's how naive I was back in 2007.

It turns out that asking people to examine prejudices is really hard. One reason it's hard is that prejudices are ubiquitous and therefore hard to examine. It's like asking people to look at air, or to look at negative space. It can be done, but it requires a little effort. American anti-intellectualism has been going on for so long that people think of it as part of the American landscape, as immutable as the purple mountains' majesty. We all "know" the central fact of the nerd/geek stereo-type: that smart people can't also be sexy, and sexy people can't also be smart. This is untrue, as we all know, but I try to point out that we all "know" it because someone taught it to us. Try-ing to get people to unlearn this untrue fact has proven to be more difficult than I imagined. But prejudices are feelings, after all, and asking people to examine their prejudices calls up strong feelings . . . on all sides of the question.

The biggest source of resistance to my central thesis has been from hip post-adolescents who believe that they have outgrown nerd/geek stereotypes. In talking with people about this book in the past two years, I have had innumerable twenty-somethings (interviewers and reporters, mostly) say to me, in some form or another, "What's the big deal? We now know nerds and geeks are cool." It's that royal *we* that always gets in the way: the twenty-something is really saying, "The anti-intellectual prejudice I had when I was in middle school has been superseded by something hip, cool, and ironic. I am now happy to dress or even act like a 'geek' because I can iron-ically embrace a vilified stereotype." To which I have replied, with varying degrees of patience, "Okay, fine, glad you finally woke up, *but you're not in middle school.*" Anti-intellectual stereotypes are important to examine because of their effect on our children. I'm a developmental psychologist: I spend a lot of time with kids, and I know that children's thinking is not like ours. Kids in seventh grade are rarely hip, cool, and ironic in the multilayered, po-mo fashion of urban reporters or media people. Kids in seventh grade think nerds are just awful, and they make life decisions accordingly. Some of those life deci-sions involve not studying science and math, which is a bad thing for them and for our country. Years later, when kids eventually get with it and learn that "nerdiness" itself is a stupid conceit, they feel a modicum of embarrassment, *but they rarely then go back and study calculus.* So, while I am happy that many hipsters have outgrown their prejudices, I still think those prejudices are a big deal.

Another objection to my claims has come from nerd-labeled people themselves. In late 2009, in a moment of crankiness, I gave an interview to a business reporter for *The New York Times* in which I said I thought the terms "nerd" and "geek" should be banned outright because of their negative effects *on kids.* It turns out that a lot of nerd-labeled people are free-speech enthusiasts, and I was pilloried again in blogs all over the world for saying that (1) nerd/geek prejudices still exist and still affect kids, and (2) we adults bear some responsibility for these stereotypes' propagation. To those who have adopted a term of derogation as a badge of honor (geek pride and all that) I say, You go, geek. But don't pretend to me that your personal achievement in overcoming prejudice is a universal achievement. Because I still talk to kids every day who tell me, "Yeah, I could be getting A's in school instead of C's, but I don't want people to think I'm a *nerd.*" I still talk to kids who want to die because other kids scream at them, literally scream at them, in the halls of junior high schools, "GET AWAY FROM ME, NERD!" because they did really well on a math test.

Despite my own efforts in this book, and despite the coolitude of the post–adolescent-prejudice crowd, the bad news is that the nerd/geek trope still exists, in school hallways and in the national media. It is the favorite of lazy journalists everywhere, people looking for a familiar hook for their stories. In this lazy world, people still think that physical beauty or sexiness and intellectual achievement are mutually exclusive. A recent example: In August 2010, a story appeared in *The New York Times* about Wisconsin congressman Paul Ryan, the new darling of the theoretical right. In this article, we learn Ryan is "fit from years of an intense exercise program called P90X" and has "hair as thick as Rod Blagojevich's (and cut in a more contemporary fashion)." Ryan "has become a regular on the cable news circuit, and a book he co-wrote about conservative politics . . . will include his picture on the cover when it comes out this fall." He sounds kinda dreamy, huh? But wait: In the next paragraph, we learn that "the inner nerd seeps through: he often sleeps on a cot in his office, says he has 'every 15-minute interval' until September scheduled, and writes up these Power-Points himself ('I really like PowerPoint')." The story could have said, "This guy has it all. . . . He works out, he looks good, and he is also smart and hardworking!" But what is being said about Ryan? He looks pretty, but on the inside he is *really* a nerd, someone who likes work and technology, and often sleeps alone. Because we all know one cannot be both sexy and smart.

Am I being too picky? Perhaps. More than one reviewer of this book said it was a "nerdy" book, meaning, I guess, detailed. But this kind of careful attention to the implications of stereotypes is routine in our culture where other harmful stereotypes are concerned: regarding racial or ethnic stereotypes, careers fall every day on complicated parsings of offhand prejudiced remarks. The nerd/geek stereotype, as harmful as it is, is allowed to pass, a state of affairs I still hope to challenge.

Still think I'm being too fussy? How about this one? An article about Ben Bernanke in *Time* magazine, in the issue in which he is named as "Person of the Year" for 2009, *begins* as follows:

> A bald man with a gray beard and tired eyes is sitting in his oversize Washington office, talking about the economy. He doesn't have a commanding presence. He isn't a mesmerizing speaker. He has none of the look-at-me swagger or listen-to-me charisma so common among men with oversize Washington offices. His arguments aren't partisan or ideological; they're methodical, grounded in data and the latest academic literature. When he doesn't know something, he doesn't bluster or bluff. He's professorial, which makes sense, because he spent most of his career as a professor.
>
> He is not, in other words, a typical Beltway power broker. He's shy. He doesn't do the D.C. dinner-party circuit; he prefers to eat at home with his wife, who still makes him do the dishes and take out the trash. Then they do crosswords or read. Because Ben Bernanke is a nerd.
>
> He just happens to be the most powerful nerd on the planet.

What do we learn about Mr. Bernanke here? More important, what do we learn about nerds? They're shy. They have no swagger, no charisma. They're henpecked (the author stopped short of describing how Mr. Bernanke's wife has him put on an apron when she "makes him do the dishes"). That's why it's so surprising when Bernanke turns out to be powerful after all. Huh. A nerd like that, Person of the Year. Will wonders never cease?

Since this book first appeared, little has changed in the nerdscape of American culture. If anything, nerd and geek stereotypes have become more ubiquitous. *The Big Bang Theory,* a network show about a bunch of intellectually gifted social misfits, is consistently ranked among the top five shows on TV. The show demonstrates that people who are gifted in science and math also love comic books, have no social skills and no sense of humor, and cannot get a girl no matter what. But they are kinda cute. The progress supposedly represented by *The Big Bang Theory* is that nerds and geeks are no longer presented as hateful or disgusting, or insane, as media depictions of mathematicians have always tended to be. Leonard and Sheldon, they're kinda cute. They're harmless. They're our *mascots*. It doesn't matter (as a recent *New York Times* article about the show points out) that many scientists feel the show is a big step in the direction of the Stone Age. It's *funny* . . . kind of like *Amos 'n' Andy* was funny. Forgive me for saying that we still have a lot of work to do.

In the two years I have spent discussing this book with others, there have been some enthusiastic supporters of my arguments. Many of those supporters are educators, people who bump up against the deleterious effects of nerd/geek stereotypes every day. They hear how kids actively discourage one another from excelling in school, especially in math and science, and they sometimes become painfully aware of how they contribute to the problem. I have talked to teachers about what works (enthusiasm and dramatic results, whether from robots or rockets) and what doesn't (apologizing for complexity: "I know this is nerdy, but stick with me here"). These discussions have been a tonic to me: people who work with kids know what I'm talking about, and take the arguments herein seriously.

And it is serious. The last two years have seen an explosion in concern among those who want to foster kids' adoption of STEM careers (science, technology, engineering, and mathematics). Consortia of businesspeople, educators, and legislators all across the country are developing models for attitude change because of the brute-force necessity of developing a technologically sophisticated workforce to bolster America's economic competitiveness in the decades ahead. And these consortia—at least the ones I have been privileged to talk to—are increasingly savvy about the effect of stereotypes on kids' career decisions. In a world where people steadfastly believe that exposure to media violence makes kids more violent, and exposure to sexualized images makes kids more sexually precocious, there is some tentative acceptance for the idea that perhaps exposure to anti-intellectual media images make kids anti-intellectual. The findings of these groups consistently support the idea that kids in middle school are the target audience: it is among this age group that attitudes about science and math are first formed and become part of kids' developing identities. That's why the San Diego Science Festival (in which I played a small part in 2009) devoted three weeks' worth of science education to middle school kids and their families. And even DARPA (Defense Advanced Research Projects Agency), the cutting-edge technology research arm of the Department of Defense, has been soliciting proposals for attitude-change programs to promote STEM career decisions. In this, I feel that I am in good company: if DARPA identifies it as a problem, it probably is.

Talking about *Nerds* in public has had its share of hilarious moments. For example, I had a lovely conversation with one editor of a hip young-women's magazine on the subject of "secret science": the editor told me nerds are now so fashionable that clubs in New York have "secret science" nights where young people gather to drink and learn about new developments in science. To which I replied, "So if it's so hip, why does it need to be called 'secret' science?" and we had a wonderful discussion about scientists and closets. And I laughed to myself over and over again when I had conversations with media folks who listened to me talk about the nerd stereotype as mean, unhelpful, false and derogatory, only to have them ask the follow-up question, "So, Dr. Anderegg. *Are you* a nerd?" I have finally come up with a standard reply: "I am a passionate devotee of Red Sox baseball and Baroque counterpoint. I have pretty good social skills and I occasionally teach research methodology and design. I am greatly enjoying learning to play golf and I love everything involving anagrams. What does that make me? You figure it out."

There have been many touching moments for me as well. These have come as I have listened, in parent groups or call-in shows, to parents who feel desperate as they observe their kids intentionally sabotaging their school grades or throwing away their extraordinary talents because of nerd/geek prejudices. And there are always the comments from regretful adults who wish they had not abandoned science and math for such stupid reasons. And there are stories from families and kids who are struggling, sometimes heroically, against prejudice in their own communities. One family contacted me after their daughter was vilified for objecting to a "tolerance" pageant at their local high school. It seems that the end of the show featured kids dressed up in costumes representing high school tribes (jock, nerd, goth, etc.), prancing around to a song indicating that "there's a place for all of us at old Westwood High" or wherever it was. The girl objected to the show, pointing out that this kind of thing just reified hurtful and harmful stereotypes: the "nerds" all had big glasses, and pocket protectors, and goofy smiles, and too-short pants . . . the whole ridiculous package. She pointed out that the dance number would be like having a pageant with costumed people acting out exaggerated racial and ethnic stereotypes, and then saying, "We're all welcome here!" But her objections fell on deaf ears; the pageant went on as planned, and she was singled out as a stick-in-the-mud, party-pooper, *intolerant* kid.

Oh, well. What can one say? If DARPA has its way, perhaps the future will be free of this kind of foolishness. But for now, just let me say it has been a great privilege to meet so many like-minded people who have generously shared their experiences with me. While we wait for DARPA to do its work, we all can continue to ask people to look, really look, at the anti-intellectual prejudices they live with every day. Attitudes can change: it takes time, but it can happen. That's what this book was all about, and that's what it's still about.

David Anderegg
West Stockbridge, Massachusetts

INTRODUCTION:
THE NERD DILEMMA

· OR ·

WHY ASHTON KUTCHER IS YOUR
KID'S WORST NIGHTMARE

Not so long ago, in the days of classic television shows like *The Twilight Zone*, people were entertained by the "alien visitor" exercise: If beings from another planet were visiting America, what would they think of us? What would they conclude about how our society works? The exercise was weird, and fun, because it invited us to look at ourselves with a fresh eye, to examine what might not otherwise draw our attention because it is so familiar. The alien visitor has gone on to be a comedy staple since then—think the Coneheads, *Mork and Mindy*, or *Third Rock from the Sun*—and although the ponderous self-examination of Rod Serling has been replaced by something much lighter, or sillier (depending on how ponderous one is feeling on any given day), the exercise is still a good one. With that in mind, I ask you, dear reader, the following question: Have you ever watched *Beauty and the Geek*? Or *The Big Bang Theory*?

Imagine you were a visitor from another planet and you

watched an episode, or (God forbid) the entire season of Ashton Kutcher's recent venture into televised "reality." If you were an alien visitor, you would learn one important thing about American culture: American earthlings come in two subgroups. There are beautiful people who appear to be hotly desired by everyone else for something called "sex" and there are ugly people who are not desired at all for the thing called "sex." And then there are intelligent people, who seem to know an awful lot, and stupid people, who seem to be, well, really stupid. And here's the really interesting part, if you're the alien visitor: *All the really intelligent people are ugly, and all the beautiful people are dumber than a box of rocks.*

A charitable alien might say, "How nice! How fair! All the good qualities human earthlings demonstrate are distributed so nicely and fairly! No one gets to be beautiful *and* smart, and no one has to be dumb *and* ugly!" A less charitable alien might say, "How nice! They will be easy to conquer because the smart ones all want to mate with the dumb ones, and therefore earthlings will never get any smarter! We won't need much more than a weed whacker to take over this whole planet!"

Whatever the extraterrestrial aliens might end up thinking, they've got a lot to mull over when they watch *Beauty and the Geek* or *The Big Bang Theory*. But my point is not about those aliens. It is about the little terrestrial aliens already in our midst: our children. Children are just like those aliens; even the cultures they are born into are alien to them. They need to make sense of the adult world, the world of their own culture, and they approach this world with alien eyes. Some of the rules are easy to learn: their native language, what to eat and what not to eat—things that are simple enough. But learning complex cultural constructs takes time and practice and maturity. And the more complicated a cultural construct is, the more time and growth it takes for kids to get it.

That's what this book is about: how kids learn the complicated constructs "nerd" and "geek." Even the subtle distinction between nerds and geeks is not easy for kids or grown-ups to learn, as we shall see. But learning the whole complex is an even larger undertaking. American kids are not born knowing what a nerd is, and what they learn and how they learn it says a tremendous amount about them and, of course, about us, the adults doing the cultural transmission. This book is about how we let kids in on the notion that beauty and brains are mutually exclusive . . . well, sort of. As I said, the notion is complicated. But this book is also about what happens when you send a complicated message to an uncomplicated recipient. What parts of the message are received, and in what order? Because kids are a lot less complicated than we are, they get the message in parts. This book is about the parts: what parts of the message kids get first, what they get later, and what effect it has on them.

If you watch *Beauty and the Geek* for a whole season (an exercise I wouldn't wish on a dog, but never mind that), you'll see that the message really does get complicated. Toward the end of the season, the "beauties," all beautiful women who appear to have IQs hovering somewhere on the basement stairs, try to teach the "geeks" something about being beautiful. And indeed, the geeks, people who look like they are allergic to every kind of soap, become somewhat more beautiful. Because all's fair in Kutcherworld, the geeks do the same for the beauties. Toward the end of the season, they try to teach the gorgeous young women to be smarter, and the gorgeous young women do indeed learn a lot of things. So one could argue that the message of the show, even for kids, is that people do not have to be stuck in their stereotypes: People can change and become multidimensional. Whether or not kids get this message is another story, as we shall see later.

Beauty and the Geek is not really so unusual; it has the formal properties of a lot of popular culture. It's actually a lot like the Berenstain Bears books for children or *The Simpsons*. Papa Bear or Homer Simpson might learn a lesson or two in the course of an episode, but by the beginning of the next episode he has reverted to his old stupid, infantile self. If he didn't revert, he wouldn't be Papa Bear or Homer Simpson. It's not a bildungsroman, and we shouldn't expect it to be, right? So what *Beauty and the Geek* might teach our little aliens is that *some* clueless, ugly, smart people can be rehabilitated, and *some* moronic sex objects can be enlightened. What *The Big Bang Theory* teaches us is that sometimes geeky guys can get a girl, but usually the less geeky guys are the ones who succeed, and when the really geeky guys get a girl, it's often an equally geeky girl. And of course, by the beginning of the next episode, people have forgotten what they learned in the last episode and they are back to their old stereotypical selves. Let's just say that no matter how uplifting the late-stage transformation, it never calls the show's basic premise—that beauty and brains are mutually exclusive—into question.

HOW NERDS ARE LIKE WASPs, EXCEPT WHEN THEY'RE NOT

So this book is about the process of stereotype acquisition and the nerd/geek stereotype in particular. But anyone writing about stereotypes needs to come clean about his own attitudes and his own positions about a particular stereotype and stereotyping in general. So, being a responsible citizen, I state my own biases here: I don't think the nerd/geek stereotype is particularly healthy for kids or for American society. I don't think kids should have to give up things they really love, even if they are nerdy or geeky things, in order to get a date. I don't think hunky scientists should have to pose for beefcake calendars just to prove there is such a thing as a hunky scientist. And I don't think kids or grown-ups should be so eager to punish "geeky" enthusiasm with shaming, even if the enthusiasm is for arcane things.

It is this last point that is most important, at least to me. I spend a lot of time with kids, and I like them because they are kids. One of the things that makes kids kids is their lack of self-consciousness, and one of the things that most distinguishes nerdy kids from nonnerdy kids is exactly this quality, as we shall see later on. One might say that the kids whom others label as really nerdy are the ones who are the last to develop the self-consciousness of adolescence or, in other words, the last to grow up. The weird enthusiasms, the willingness to cooperate with adults, the lack of social skills—all these things seem nerdy and pathetic to sophisticated, self-conscious teenagers. But nerdiness has its own charms. We might even stop to celebrate the fact that many of our religious traditions recount that we are all descended from Adam and Eve, the First Nerds, who, when they disobeyed, got a lot more self-conscious—and a lot more miserable.

Despite my biases, I don't expect the nerd/geek stereotype to wither away anytime soon. And I certainly don't intend to scold my readers into shamefaced silence and expect them never to use the hated terms again. Contemporary social-science research has demonstrated conclusively over the last twenty years that having stereotypes (i.e., knowing the content of stereotypes) is practically universal. It has also shown that people who wish not to be biased and who do not act in a biased fashion can be shown to act according to stereotypes when those stereotypes are unconsciously cued. Stereotyping is a universal feature of human information-processing, probably derived from the need of our ancestors living on the grassy plains of Africa to reduce complex information relatively quickly when survival was at stake. So although I think nerd/geek stereotypes are not generally good, don't worry; this book is not intended to be a sermon. All stereotypes reduce their bearers' humanity, no matter what they are. But there you go: Being human isn't all that pretty.

The nerd/geek stereotype is, of course, a good one for study because it is used so frequently. People have not been shamed into silence about using it, because it is seen as a fun, harmless stereotype: It is negative and pejorative, but it is applied to people who will be just fine, or maybe even privileged, anyway, so who cares if their feelings are hurt? Nerds and geeks will end up ruling the world anyway, right? One need only look to Nerd Exhibit A, Bill Gates, to get the picture. So taking them down a peg now is only fair, or maybe just an expression of a not-so-unconscious envy, a subject to which we will also return. In this sense nerds are very much like WASPs or "yuppies," two other complicated stereotypes kids need to be instructed about if they are going to participate in grown-up American culture.

Let's take the WASP stereotype, for example. When you

think about it, it's pretty complicated. WASPs are, like nerds, not immediately visible to kids, at least not to white kids. They are not of a different color, so their differences are not immediately apparent to a kid. Kids need to learn how to recognize them; how else to explain the mysterious popularity of *The Official Preppy Handbook*? Kids do not immediately know that the following things *do* actually go together: blond hair, madras pants, a passion for wooden boats, attendance at Episcopalian churches, locked jaws, a genuine unironic taste for foods cooked in aspic, riding lessons, playing squash, bad cooking, islands off the coast of New England, gin, and an ethical code the first principle of which is "Never spend capital." We know who they are, and we mock them freely, even now. For a contemporary example, we might look to Lorelei's parents on *Gilmore Girls*. We can all use the term "WASP" without worrying about seeming to be prejudiced or mean, because WASPs can look out for themselves. (Indeed, if the stereotype is correct, they are very good at it.) But learning the stereotype can take time, especially if one grows up in Iowa or Arkansas, where WASPs aren't exactly a dime a dozen: It takes practice to learn that when people say "the vineyard," they mean *the* Vineyard (as in Martha's Vineyard), not just any vineyard.

Yuppies, of course, are even more mysterious. Yuppies are worse than WASPs, execrable in every way, but who the hell are they? Young urban professionals, okay. The term is used in such a protean fashion that it is almost meaningless; listing the stigmas of yuppiedom, as we can easily do for WASPdom, is a very difficult project to undertake with any degree of certainty.[*] It is easy to insult yuppies, of course, because the membership group is so mysterious that no one quite knows how to decide who is one . . . and therefore one can deny (at least to oneself) group membership. Indeed, this term may have come and gone, because its referent is so vague that people just can't understand it or because the implication of conspicuous consumption is so widespread that everyone is one.

The nerd/geek stereotype is kind of like these, because it is complex and not immediately visible; it requires some training. But as is not the case with "WASP" and "yuppie," kids apply the terms "nerd" and "geek" to one another. They know it is a bad thing to be, and they know they don't want to be one, even before they know what it is. They know from other kids' intonation that it is a term of scorn, and therefore something to be avoided. It is, of course, a painful moment in the life of all kids when they hear the term applied to themselves and realize that it fits. But it is also painful for kids whom the term does not fit; those kids have to spend a lot of time trying to figure out if they are nerds or geeks, and they have another thing about which to be vigilant.

Take a trip down your own memory lane to when you were a kid and heard a new derogatory or illicit term. For me, the

---

[*]But that doesn't stop people from applying the term! In my home county in western Massachusetts, a place where old-time farmers and laborers are being slowly squeezed out by transplants from big cities (like me) and by seasonal onslaughts of tourists, the term means something like "not one of us." When I went to my local farm stand, the kid working there noticed my fascination with what was then new to me, a purple potato, and said blithely, "Oh, you'll love that—that's a real yuppie potato!"

prototype was when I was nine, and a fourteen-year-old sister of one of my friends said to us, "You don't want people to think you're a *snerd*, do you?" The way she said it made it perfectly clear that it was a terrible thing to be, but neither my friend nor I knew what it meant. Of course, we begged for enlightenment, and we were told with perfect clarity that a "snerd" was a boy who went around sniffing girls' bicycle seats. We were both *way* too embarrassed to ask why anyone would do that; at nine, I hadn't a clue. The term I remember from way back then has changed, of course. Now the Internet will tell a kid with perfect authority that someone who goes around sniffing girls' bicycle seats is a "gink," or a "quibbie," or a "snurge"; it is also an activity associated with a "nerd." All I remember is being confused, a little ashamed, and determined not to be one of *those*.

American childhood is full of such moments. Indeed, shame is part and parcel of what it is like to be a kid. Grown-ups are well insulated from shame, and because it is such an awful thing to feel, they avoid it at all costs. But to go one step beyond the ancient television host, kids feel ashamed about the darnedest things. That, too, is what this book is about.

TALKING TO KIDS ABOUT STEREOTYPES

I am a clinical child psychologist and a college teacher in developmental psychology, so I know something about kids. I began my career in psychology thirty years ago talking to kids, and watching kids talk to one another, about their friendships, and since then I have talked to kids about all kinds of things: superheroes, how to remember things, death, being Good and being Bad, disease, parents, geometry, music, magic . . . all kinds of things. And I am privileged to be able to talk to kids about all kinds of things in a sheltered setting where they usually feel comfortable enough to open up. But talking to kids about stereotypes is not easy. That shame thing, for instance, makes a lot of kids, especially the younger ones, reticent. They think it's not okay to talk about mean things. It's kind of like swearing, and they think they're not supposed to. Speaking to six- or seven-year-olds when they are first developing the nerd/geek stereotype is interesting, but it is mighty hard to do. They get embarrassed and balky if they have heard the words, because frequently all they know is that they are bad. (They sure don't know what a pocket protector is or an SAT score.) But if they haven't heard the words, it is not at all nice being the bearer of bad news. When kids haven't really heard or thought about the terms "nerd" and "geek," no grown-up, me included, wants to introduce them. Any kid being grilled about nerds by a grown-up will ask himself or herself, Why am I being questioned about this, and why is it so important? The first thing kids will want to do is go out and learn all they can (from their friends) about nerds and geeks.

Anthropologists know all about this and try to avoid it whenever possible: changing the phenomenon under observation by the act of observation. It makes the project, interviewing younger kids about the concept, difficult. But it is also more than a little unsettling from a moral point of view. If part of the experience of nerds is that they are unself-conscious, a good long interview on the topic can spoil all that in a second. It's kind of like being the snake in the Garden of Eden: introducing self-consciousness where it does not heretofore exist. It's not a nice thing to do.

So the interviews with kids in this book tend to be with older kids who are in high school or college, who all have been well indoctrinated in the ways of the nerd by then, have lots to say on the subject, and remember enough of their childhood to recall when they started thinking about these issues. The reported interviews with younger kids arose mostly in casual conversation about other things and tended to be brief to avoid that snake-in-the-Garden thing. But those in a position to overhear kids when they are on the playground or when they are in the backseat of the car will recognize the truth in the fragments I have been able to provide.

THE FULL-DISCLOSURE PART

Full disclosures of potential conflicts of interest are all the rage on the op-ed pages these days, so why not here? Readers may want to know, is this book just some sort of special pleading? Is it the work of some raging nerd seeking revenge in his own understated, nerdy way? Don't you deserve to know if I am myself a nerd?

Happy to disclose, but it all depends on whom you ask. As noted in the following chapters, some people, especially young people, adopt a broad definition and define a nerd as anyone who wears glasses, on the theory that anyone could wear contacts if he chose to, so wearing glasses must be some sort of badge of nerdity. In that case, I am indeed a nerd; I have never been able to get used to contacts. And in a historical sense, I have certainly done some pretty nerdy things: In my fourth-grade class play, I played the part of the Dictionary. I wore a cardboard box spray-painted black with the word "Dictionary" in white letters across the front while I went around helping kids by defining words for them.* I don't remember being called a nerd, but I think my classmates and I were just a little too young and, besides, the term then was "brainiac."

In high school, I was saved by the counterculture: Just when I was sinking into terminal nerdiness as a member of the high school debate team *and* an oboe player in the high school band, I discovered hippiedom. My long hair and enthusiastic embrace of hippie clothes and politics saved me from the approval I once had from nearby adults, the pathognomic sign of the high school nerd. And by the time I got to college, of course, it no longer mattered. So when I write of nerdiness, I know whereof I speak, although I usually spared myself the overt hostility of my classmates by being crafty. So revenge, dear reader, is not on the agenda. If it's revenge you want, go elsewhere. (I can direct you to a lot of websites where pissed-off nerds and geeks call for Armageddon in the never-ending war on jocks, but I advise you to stay away if you want a good night's sleep.)

---

*But I wised up. In sixth grade, I finagled myself into the role of casting director for the class play about the Trojan War and cast myself as Hector. Not exactly believable, but an attempt at reputation repair nonetheless.

THE PLAN OF THIS BOOK

In the following pages, then, I hope to address the question: If you were a visitor from another planet, how would you *really* understand popular culture? In the first four chapters, we take a look at the current and historical versions of the nerd/geek stereotype. What do we think nerds are, and what do our kids think nerds are? We'll inspect the landscape and try to map the cultural definitions of "nerd" and "geek" and then compare them with kids' understandings of these concepts. As we shall see, we get two very different maps. We'll also look at the concept cross-culturally and historically to find out why it is so uniquely American. In chapters 5 through 9, we'll look at the specifics of the nerd/geek stereotype, at least as defined by "Are you a nerd?" self-tests on the Internet. We'll consider the Five Foundations of Nerdiness: Nerds are, by definition: (a) unsexy, (b) interested in technology, (c) uninterested in their personal appearance, (d) enthusiastic about stuff that bores everybody else, and (e) persecuted by nonnerds who are sometimes known as jocks. We'll look at research data and talk to nerdy and nonnerdy kids to find out what they think about the Five Foundations, and we'll ask whether these attributes really go together at all. In the last chapter, we'll think about what it all means. Is this something we can, or should, change? If we can't change the stereotype, can we mitigate some of its bad effects? Or should we embrace our inner Kutcher and have fun picking on people who will be our future masters while we still can? Perhaps, at the end, we can send our alien visitors back to their home planet a little more enlightened than when they arrived.

1.

THE FIELD GUIDE
TO NERDS

· OR ·

WHY NERDS ARE
SO GAY

It started out simply enough: All I did was go to a toy store. It was an old-fashioned toy store, the chock-full, one-of-everything kind that predates today's full-of-expensive-beeping-plastic-toy superstores. It had toy soldiers, beautifully made farm animals, dolls of every description, an electric train running in figure-eights in a corner, science kits, and balls and jacks—a kids' paradise. I was there to pick up a present for a nephew, wishing my kids were still young enough to enjoy this store the way they used to. And there on the wall with trick sunglasses you can use to look behind you, Groucho glasses, and the glasses with the eyeballs on springs was something very, very creepy.

The package featured a fat young man wearing a *Star Trek* costume and a pair of very thick glasses, the kind that used to be called, in a different era, "Coke-bottle glasses." He was clearly a man, not a child, because he had an unappealing stubble. He was proudly holding a Palm Pilot and, oddly (given what was to come), wearing a wedding ring on his left hand. The package was labeled "Deluxe NERD Glasses" and, indeed, it contained a pair of plastic glasses with round black frames and very thick lenses just like the ones the young man in the picture was wearing. These are glasses one wears to make oneself look like a nerd. But this being a toy store and me being a developmental psychologist, I found myself wondering how little kids would know what a nerd is. After all, the package contains a standard warning: "Choking hazard. Small parts. Not suitable for children under 3 years." This item is apparently so appealing to little kids that we need to be warned: The desperate three-year-olds have to wait until they are four to wear their nerd glasses. But when they are four, what will they understand about nerds?

Happily for the little consumer, there is a "Nerd Test" on the back of the package. This test is one that can be scored, like the self-tests in *Cosmopolitan,* so it is supposed to be fun. Here's how fun it is.

SCORING THE NERD TEST: *Each "yes" answer is worth three points. Total number of points determines your percentage of nerdiness, up to 100 percent. You get one point for reading this far.*

Oh, okay, I said to myself. I get it. Reading, even reading a fun test you're supposed to be reading to have the fun, is an indicator of something creepy. This is a fun toy that insults you for being interested in it. Then the fun really begins.

1. Has anyone ever called you a nerd?
2. Did you skip a grade in elementary school?
3. Was your SAT math score 600 or more?
4. Can you figure out anagrams without a piece of paper?
5. Did you try to figure out if the last question was an anagram?
6. Did you letter in high school for academics or band?
7. Did you have your first drink on your twenty-first birthday? . . .
17. Do you know at least one of these languages? perl, COBOL, C, C+, C++, FORTRAN.
18. Was your last "intimate relationship" in a chat room?
19. Do you own a fanny pack or a pocket protector? . . .
21. Do you consider chess a sport? . . .
30. Have you ever told a joke about chemistry or physics?

By now my score was way over the top, but that's not the point here. The point is, the test makes it clear that this a test for adults—presumably children under three, or maybe just over three, have not yet taken their SAT tests or had their twenty-first birthday—so it is supposed to be amusing to adults. It's a novelty, not really a toy. But since it's in a toy store on the rack with all the other things that little kids also think are cool (come to think of it, maybe it's just the nerdy kids who like the sunglasses that let you look behind yourself and that's why they're in the same section of the store), it is also a vehicle for indoctrination. It tells kids what nerds are in case they don't yet know.

What kids learn from the nerd test, in combination with the picture of the nerd on the front, is that being a nerd has several components. As adults, we are familiar with these components, so familiar, in fact, that they are below the radar of analytic thought. Nerds just are, and we all know what they are. As I hope to show, our confidence on this point may be misplaced. We adults don't actually know what they are: Published instances of "nerd" and its close cousin, "geek," reveal protean terms that mean so many different things that their meaning becomes diffuse; they have become like "yuppie" or "middle-class," terms that don't really mean anything without more precise definition. We adults all think we know what the nerd test questions are meant to teach: that nerds are smart, especially in math, and also physically repulsive. They don't drink as much as other young people, and they don't have sex except over the Internet. They are interested in things that bore the crap out of nonnerds, things like chess, *Star Trek*, anagrams, and band. And, as the fanny pack and pocket protectors demonstrate, they are more interested in practicality than they are in looking cool. Most important, we know, as question 1 strongly implies, that the term is an insult. We all know these things because we've already been subjected to years and years of this kind of propaganda.

But what do kids make of all this? After all, "nerd" is a pretty complex social category. It is like other prejudicial labels and also not like them. Skin color, for example, is pretty obvi-

ous to kids, and although acquiring social stereotypes or prejudices takes time, it is a little different in the case of people who
are visually identifiable. Little white kids can, and do, wonder,
if there are ways other than skin color or facial features that
make black or Asian kids different, because those kids are different from themselves. But little kids do not have any natural
curiosity about nerds, because nerds are not readily identifiable to little kids. Little kids don't see someone who looks like
the guy on the "Deluxe NERD Glasses" package and naturally
wonder, to themselves, what kind of person that is. In this
sense, nerds are like "gays": Kids hear about them, but they
don't really know what they are, they don't *see* them. They might
be anybody, because they do not wear any visible stigmas. In fact,
as we shall see, little kids' concepts of nerds and gays overlap a
great deal, a fact that contributes greatly to the lingering animosity toward nerds among adults.

The reason kids need nerd tests is to teach them how to
recognize nerds and, even more important, how to recognize
nerdiness in themselves. Because, of course, this is why there
are so many nerd self-tests: The question "Are you a nerd?"
implies that you might be one and not even know it. Nerds are
famous for their unself-consciousness. If nerds were self-
conscious, they wouldn't be so prone to pocket protectors and
fanny packs and all those other things that make them look so
nerdy. The reason we need so many nerd self-tests is to save
the poor nerds from themselves, because really nerdy people
are those who, when asked, "Are you a nerd?" will answer, hon-
estly, "Gee, I don't know." And we all want our kids to be saved
from that particularly cruel fate.

NERDS AND GEEKS: SAME OR DIFFERENT?

Let's just start with the basics: What exactly *is* a nerd? What better place to turn for a definition of a folk concept than Wikipedia, the repository of all folk wisdom? Wikipedia tells us that a nerd is "a stereotypical or archetypal designation." It "refers to somebody who passionately pursues intellectual or esoteric interests such as books and video games rather than having a social life, participating in organized sports or other mainstream activities. The Merriam-Webster definition is an 'unstylish, unattractive, or socially inept person; especially: one slavishly devoted to intellectual or academic pursuits.'" Thank you, Wiki, for providing your own and the Merriam-Webster versions—and, might I say, how very nerdy of you to do so.

But before we turn to the question of how kids come to understand the meaning of "nerd," we have to stop and talk about geeks. The terms "nerd" and "geek" are practically synonymous in some contexts and slightly differentiated in others. Since there is really no such thing as a nerd or a geek, we can't do what many scientists do: We can't find the prototypical member of the species and then use that prototype to define all the central characteristics. We can't really answer with any finality the question about whether nerds and geeks are really two variants of the same thing, like Baltimore and northern orioles. In fact, we might observe that this is, in itself, a geeky question.*

---

*Scientists are always asking these kinds of questions. It is, in fact, the attention to specificity that makes science science and also marks it in the eyes of

We can only point to usage to see if people use the terms synonymously, and here we can observe only that some do and some don't. Geek self-tests are an awful lot like nerd self-tests: There is the emphasis on intelligence, technical knowledge, social awkwardness, and physical repulsiveness that adheres in both concepts. Here's one example, from a T-shirt seen on a college sophomore. The headline is "You know you're a geek when," and the illustration is a hand in the famous *Star Trek* position, the weird two-finger V thing they all did when they said to one another, "Live long and prosper." The T-shirt reads as follows:

You know you're a geek when

You have endless debates on who was a better captain,
   Kirk or Picard.
You own more black clothing than Marilyn Manson.
You carry a backpack full of collectible card games.
Your favorite day of the month is new-comic day.
Your diet consists of soda, snack chips, and pizza.
Your friends and family use you as tech support.
Deodorant is as foreign a concept as toothpaste or
   mouthwash.
You've played a video game for more than twelve hours
   straight.
Your mom is the only woman to ever see the inside of
   your bedroom.

kids as the domain of the geek. But as we shall see, some contexts are
geekier than others.

When your parents are worried, they call the local
  comic or computer store.
You buy two of the same action figure, one for display
  and one for "the collection."
You own a PC, a PDA, a PS2, a DVD, and an MP3
  player but not a C-A-R.
You've dressed as a movie or comic character, and it
  wasn't Halloween.
You have a shrine to Stan Lee, Gene Roddenberry, or
  Isaac Asimov somewhere in your home.
You have the comic-book store on speed-dial.
You've written an angry letter to George Lucas pointing
  out all the flaws in the new trilogy.
You know more URLs than girls' phone numbers.
You've waited months to see the latest comic-book
  movie adaptation just so you can tell everyone how
  "it sucks compared to the comic."

There are different emphases—apparently geeks read more comics than nerds—but the underlying concepts are still there: Geeks, like nerds, are interested in technology and also are physically repulsive, in this case actually odiferous because they don't wear deodorant. And they certainly don't have much of a sex life; the only women they have in their rooms are their moms, and they know more about the Internet than they do about girls. So how can we tell if these geeks are the same as nerds?

Let's go back to the Wiki. On the topic of differences between nerds and geeks, the Wiki says: "Pundits and observers dispute the relationship of the terms 'nerd' and 'geek' to one another, as many use the words synonymously. Some view the geek as a less technically skilled nerd. Others view the exact opposite. The lines between geek and nerd are often thin and ill-defined"; however, the consensus is that "a 'geek' is a person who obsesses in one area or another, whereas a 'nerd' is a highly intelligent person who is very scholarly and does well in many domains such as math, science, computing, etc. Nerds are more associated with obsessive knowledge. For example a Star Trek nerd (or *Trekkie*) is someone who could tell you extremely trivial details about Star Trek and may be likely to watch the show on a daily basis or go to Star Trek conventions." Far be it from me to disagree with the repository of world knowledge, but on this one, Wiki, I disagree. The Wiki may be biased in some respects anyway, at least on this topic, because, as a presumably nerd- or geek-authored document, it deemphasizes the unpleasant aspects of nerds and geeks that appear in every self-test and T-shirt known to American humankind.

Popular culture does, indeed, offer innumerable instances in which the terms are used synonymously. Take, for example, *Cargo* magazine, a publication for trendy young male shoppers, which in one issue features an item on "nerd shirts" with the subtitle "Get Your Geek On." Or consider the hip young novelist Jonathan Lethem's volume of autobiographical writing *The Disappointment Artist*, in which he identifies himself as a nerd. Except he doesn't. The book jacket's description of one particular essay refers to Lethem as a nerd, but in the essay itself, he uses the word "geek." It is not an accident that

Lethem does not use "nerd" in his own words; "geek" is now more likely to be used when people describe themselves, because it is slightly less pejorative than "nerd." In some circles it is now okay to be a geek, and the term "geek chic" has entered contemporary parlance to reflect the fact that many high school kids think it is totally uncool to be a geek until they get to college and they discover there are really cool people who describe themselves as geeks, like Tina Fey or Moby. There are nonprofits like GeekCorps and websites like GeekCulture that celebrate geekdom, but celebrations of nerddom are much harder to find. In my own reading of popular culture, it looks like the term "nerd" lays a subtle emphasis on the pathologically unself-conscious, physically repulsive end of the terminological spectrum, while "geek" lays a subtle emphasis on the bearer as a repository of boring arcane knowledge, especially technical knowledge.* And since being a possessor of boring arcana is slightly less undesirable than being physically repulsive, the term "geek" is the lesser of two evils when it comes to self-description.

But there are plenty of instances in which these distinctions are lost. In a recent *New York Times* article, A. O. Scott wrote about the recent popularity of movies based on comic books. It was entitled "Revenge of the Nerds," although the article itself was about comic-book fanatics, those we might more precisely call geeks, but then he goes on to describe

---

*One version of the distinction, provided by a college student of mine: Nerds are the ones who don't go to the party so they can stay home and do homework; geeks bring their homework to the party.

these comic-book fanatics as losers and misfits, so maybe he really does mean they're nerds. Since the terms are so elastic, one can get away with using them interchangeably, and since there is no cultural referent for "Revenge of the Geeks," I guess if they're getting revenge, they must be nerds. We might suggest that, although the concept is the same, when it's about appearance, the word is "nerd" and when it's about intelligence, the word is "geek." And when it's about insulting someone, it's a little more likely to be "nerd." Of course, as with all stereotypes, we would expect local variation (the Wiki suggests usage differences between the East and West Coasts) and generational shift. Younger people might not mean the same thing older people do when they use the same term. For example, very few of my college students know something that all my age-mates know: which negative racial stereotype goes with the word *watermelon*. And yet they all seem to know, as my age-mates did, which one goes with *pimp*.

Another approach to terminological clarity might be that afforded by etymology; at least it seems promising, until we start looking. The history of the terms *nerd* and *geek* sheds little light on their current usages, or how they came to mean what they now mean. The word "nerd" first appeared in 1950, in a book by Dr. Seuss, *If I Ran the Zoo*, where it referred to just another in a long list of fantastic creatures: "And then, just to show them, I'll sail to Ka-Troo, and bring back an IT-KUTCH, a PREEP, and a PROO, a NERKLE, a NERD, and a SEERSUCKER, too." The first appearance in print in its current sense appeared soon thereafter. In a 1951 *Newsweek* article, "nerd" made its journalistic debut: "In Detroit, someone who once would be called a drip or a square is now, regrettably, a nerd, or in a less severe case, a scurve." Two etymological sources have been given wide currency: one, that the word started as an acronym for Northern Electric Research and Development, an Ottawa lab founded in 1959. The other origin tale is that "nerd" began as a joke: the original spelling was "knurd," or "drunk" spelled backward. A collegiate knurd, then, was the opposite of a collegiate drunk, especially at Rensselaer Polytechnic Institute, whose alums frequently claim their alma mater as the term's birthplace. Whatever the origin, professional and lay etymologists give credit to the television show *Happy Days*, which ran from 1974 to 1984, for spreading the term like a toxic virus. Henry Winkler's character, the Fonz, used it liberally in its current sense, and the rest, so to speak, is history.

The word *geek* is far older, but how it acquired its present meaning is also obscure. It seems to be derived from *geck,* a Low German or Dutch term for a fool or a simpleton. The term appears in Shakespeare's *Twelfth Night*:

> *Why have you suffer'd me to be imprison'd,*
> *Kept in a dark house, visited by the priest,*
> *And made the most notorious geck and gull*
> *That e'er invention play'd on? tell me why.*

Centuries after Shakespeare, in America, the term was used to describe circus performers or sideshow freaks, including and especially those who amazed their audiences by biting the heads off live chickens. Some etymologists point to the 1946 novel *Nightmare Alley* by William Lindsay Gresham as a source for wider currency of "geek" in the sideshow sense. In the 1960s, when "freak" was in wide currency to denote a drug user or a hippie, "geek" began to be used as a synonym, probably because of the rhyme. But no one knows for sure (no one knows anything for sure in questions of etymology) how the term moved from describing simpletons, carnies, or hippies to its current use.

Another way to understand nerds and geeks is to become aware of what nerds and geeks are not. There is a complementary stereotype that helps us to define what nerds and geeks are, because it sums up what they lack: Nerds and geeks are, by definition, not jocks. Jocks are self-conscious, socially skilled, attractive, popular, and, of course, athletic, and nerds and geeks are none of these things. The terminological opposition is based on the "real" opposition of these groups of people in high school, and in this historical sense, the terms are just labels for tribal identifications of old. So Sarah Vowell, in her book *The Partly Cloudy Patriot*, can describe the Bush-versus-Gore election as a "classic" nerd-versus-jock confrontation. Scott Simon, on National Public Radio, when reporting on the steroids-in-baseball hearings in Congress, can describe the hearings as the jocks versus the nerds. (Forgetting for the moment that politics is the career choice of many more jocks than nerds, nerds are the behind-the-scenes Karl Roves while the George Bushes are out front for the photo ops.) There is a logic here that defies reality, and the logic is, *nerd* and *geek* are simply other terms for "not-jocks."

The facts of this matter are irrelevant. Indeed, like all stereotypes, these stereotypes mostly defy logic and reality. That's another thing that makes them hard for kids to learn:

They contain a lot of things that are observably untrue. In order for kids to master these stereotypes, they need to assent to the myth that intelligence and athleticism are mutually exclusive. The truth is, as behavioral scientists have shown for a hundred years, brains and physical coordination are very likely to occur in the same people because they spring from the same roots, good prenatal health and good postnatal physical caretaking. But the facts are not what kids learn as they grow up. Kids learn that nerds and geeks are pretty much the same and that they're both the opposite of jocks. Kids learn the erroneous conviction that people can be one or the other or neither, but *they cannot be both*. And they learn the bedrock principle that nerds and geeks are bad, and jocks are good.

THE GOOD, THE BAD, AND THE NERDY

I use "good" and "bad" advisedly. The first question that occurs to kids, when they encounter the term "nerd" for the first time, is: Are nerds bad or good? As I hope to show, this is how kids think, but more and more it is how adults think as well. Living in twenty-first-century America makes me glad I studied history in college: I stumbled into the "culture wars" already knowing what *Manichean* means, so I'm already a step ahead when I read the op-ed page of *The New York Times*.*

---

*The prophet Mani lived and preached in Persia in the third century A.D. He preached a doctrine of dualism, or the opposition of light and darkness. Although Manicheans were pronounced heretics by early Christian bishops,

There are probably all sorts of ineffable reasons why our culture has devolved into one in which nuance is dead. We could blame politicians or religious fundamentalists who choose to frame every argument in simplistic moral terms, but we need to ask why such simplicity meets such a sympathetic response from a presumably educated public. In other words, when we're looking for someone to blame for the modern Manichean style, we might start by looking in the mirror. After all, politicians and religious leaders are not the only authors of this trend. My favorite example from the world of pop culture is the late and unlamented reality show *Are You Hot or Not?* because it demonstrated the fallacy of Manichean categories so clearly. The show, in case you missed it, featured all sorts of good-looking people of both sexes, parading in front of the judges and studio audience, who would, within three seconds, decide whether the contestants were "hot" or "not." Even in those three seconds, one could discern that there was quite a range and that two categories were totally inadequate to capture the practically infinite variety on parade. Most of the "nots" were pretty attractive, albeit in some interesting or quirky ways, but since there were only two choices, they were instantly out of the running. The "hots" were subsequently worshipped, and the "nots" scorned. The show was totally shameless—it also featured C-list celebrity judges using laser pointers to draw attention to the contestants' unattractive physical features—but obviously satisfying on some deep human level.

---

some historians see Manichean influences entering Christian doctrine through the work of Saint Augustine, who was a born a Manichean.

That level is, of course, the level of children. Children learn to make simple categorical distinctions at first and more elaborate ones later. This was elegantly demonstrated in the early part of the twentieth century by the Gestalt psychologist Heinz Werner, who showed that all categories in the process of formation start with simple distinctions that are enlarged and integrated over time. These simple categorizations are usually overinclusive and crude. They are the source of charming productions of child language that adults cherish precisely because they are so childlike. When children are first learning to categorize animals, they might call everything with fur a "bowwow": It is obvious that they are learning by dividing the world into the simple categorical distinction "living things with fur" and "living things without fur." So cats, bears, and sheep might all be called "bowwows" at first, until the finer distinctions are made and labeled and put into proper relationships with each other. This is how children think, and this is how we all thought when we were children: *First we divide the world into two parts.*

And next we give each part a value. It is a simple, natural way of childish thinking to assign a value to everything, something we forget as we become more mature and realize that many things, especially abstract concepts, are pretty much value-neutral. For example, little kids always have positive or negative feelings about numbers: They will say they like 4 or 7, say, or hate 6 or 9. (This lingers on in many adults' feelings about their own "lucky numbers," but most adults don't have a positive or negative feeling about every number, the way a lot of children do.) Children have favorite colors and least favorite colors; they like some words and hate others. Very little, in the developing world of childhood, is neutral. Indeed, in my work as a clinical psychologist, I frequently try to help kids develop out of the childish worldview in which everything is liked or disliked. Immature middle schoolers, for example, frequently suffer in school because they refuse to do homework for a teacher they don't like. They need to learn that they can, and should, do their homework for teachers whether they like them or not. They also need to learn that, although it might be difficult, it is still possible to learn something from someone they don't like at all. Learning something "good" from a "bad" person—that's a real move in the direction of mature thought.

But thinking in black-and-white categorizations is still very satisfying for adults, because it is familiar: It is the way we all thought when we were kids, and it is the way we still think when we are stressed out or overloaded with information. Adults, when not stressed out or overloaded, have much more ability to handle shades of gray; this is why we can appreciate concepts like "geek chic" or the notion that nerds might indeed be, in some way, cool. It is always the older kids, like kids in late high school or college, or the precocious younger kids, who start to articulate a concept like "geek chic" because it is complex; it is a way of saying, "You know those kids we thought were despicable? Well, there might, just maybe, be something about them that is not despicable." But the shades of gray are interesting to kids precisely because they overlay a concept that has been, so far, black and white: What kids learn first is that being a nerd or a geek is bad, really bad. Later on, they might learn that there are some nerds or geeks who are not quite so bad, or good *and* bad. But the default conviction, the one kids return to when things get complicated, alas, is that nerds are bad.

We know this is the default conviction because we can see it appear in times of trouble. When people are suffering from severe anxiety or fear, they usually regress to simpler ways of thinking. We might think of this as battlefield thinking: There is little or no time for subtlety or self-questioning when you are being shot at. You just need to know who's a good guy and who's a bad guy. In times of national emergency, or *felt* national emergency, rigid black-and-white thinking always makes an appearance. After 9/11, the United States went through a brief period of extreme xenophobic feeling that extended to anyone perceived as Middle Eastern–appearing, even Hindus and Sikhs. And after the Columbine massacre in 1999, parents and school officials across the country started persecuting nerds and geeks in the same manner. They were "sort of" like the Columbine killers: smart, computer-savvy, social outcasts. . . . It didn't take long for people to connect those dots and start expelling outlier kids from schools throughout the country. In this massive psychic regression, the old categories of childhood thinking were once again revealed: We needed to know who was a good guy and who was a bad guy, and nerds and geeks seemed to be mostly in the enemy camp.

This is a prejudice unlike any other in American culture at present. Enlightened adults would not dream of instructing kids in any other negative social stereotype and tell themselves it's okay to do it because the kids will outgrow it. We would not, for example, teach kids every false ugly thing that is said about African-Americans or Hispanics and then hope that when they grow up they will figure out that those things aren't really true. We work hard to combat prejudice before it ever gets started, because we know how hard it is to eradicate once it *does* get started. How would we react if we walked into a toy store and saw, for example, an Afro wig in a package with a self-test on the back that asks: "Are you a nigger?" It would be appalling, and totally off-limits. But when it comes to nerds and geeks, we pretend it's all in good fun; we adults know that nerds and geeks are okay and that in fact we can't live without them, so we think it's okay to make fun of them. We act like it's all in good fun to communicate to our kids that people who are smart and do well in school and like science fiction and computers are also people who smell bad and look ugly and are so repulsive that they are not allowed to have girlfriends. And then we wonder why it's so hard to motivate kids to do well in school.

WHAT THE KIDS SAY

Talking to kids about nerds and nerdiness is always a difficult enterprise. As a well-meaning adult, the last thing I want to do is to sit kids down and introduce them to a poisonous concept that they might not yet have heard. If they don't know the term yet, I want to protect their innocence as long as possible. The age of deepest nerd anxiety is middle school, roughly ages eleven to fourteen, but in an era in which every cultural territory previously owned by teenagers is being relentlessly jammed down the throats of tweens, it is difficult to know, now, who is hip to nerds and who is not. But as a child therapist, I get to talk to kids all day about whatever is on their minds, and anxieties about nerds and nerdiness are never too far away when talking to kids of a certain age.

Adam is in the first grade, and for a first-grader, he's pretty immature. When I ask him what a nerd is, he squirms in his chair and says, "I don't want to talk about that." How come? "It makes me sad." With a little gentle prodding, it turns out that he doesn't know what a nerd is; he thinks it's something like a geek. He doesn't know what a geek is either, but he thinks it might be something like "freak." And he doesn't know what a "freak" is either, but he does know that some kids on the playground called him a freak in a very angry way, so it was obviously something bad. He doesn't know anything about nerdiness or geekiness except the valence: in the black-and-white world of his childhood, these words are *bad*.

Max, a fourth-grade student, sits in my office talking about school. He is very smart, with two highly educated professional parents, and they are worried about (among other things) his lack of interest in doing his homework. As we are talking, he remarks in passing that there is a kid in his class who is a real nerd. "Really?" I say. "What do you mean by that?" He looks at me with disdain: Don't I know what a nerd is? Yes, I think I do, I say, but I want to know what he thinks. A nerd, he says with conviction, is someone who always does what he is told. A nerd does well in school because that's what teachers and parents want. A nerd is, to Max, the same thing as a suck-up: a kid who is eager to please the authorities. And whatever else Max knows about nerds, he knows he doesn't want to be one.

I have heard this time and time again from kids in late elementary school. Whatever the etymological history for kids, the conceptual history of nerds and nerdiness has a clear and distinguished pedigree: The concept "nerd" is an extension or elaboration of the venerable term "baby." First- and second-graders (and also some precocious younger kids) are in unanimous agreement about one thing: how repulsive it is to be a "baby." A baby is someone who needs too much adult help. A baby is a whiner, a kid who cries too easily. But he is also a kid who seeks adult help or intervention too readily. A baby is a kid who is more attached to adults and their good opinions than the normal first-grader should be. It is a common playground epithet and one that is almost always delivered with contempt.

So when Max tells me with conviction that a nerd is someone who wants to please adults, the contempt he expresses is old, borrowed contempt. It is the contempt for "babies," only now instead of crying to the teacher when they aren't allowed to play kick ball, they're demonstrating their "babyness" by doing well on their homework and raising their hands to answer every question. This is the sense of nerd and nerdiness that also bleeds over into "gay" and "gayness." Kids who are nerdy or "gay" are kids who are too invested in the good opinion of adults.

Take, for example, the case of Peter, a ten-year-old whose progressive mother was totally confused by his constant use of "gay" as a negative epithet. Peter used the term on his younger siblings, who then used it on everyone they knew, and their mother was extremely distressed. As a native of Denmark, she could not understand why kids in the States were antihomosexual so early, and she wondered what it meant that Peter was preoccupied with homosexuality. So we all sat together, and

Peter explained to her, with very little help on my part, what "gay" meant. It meant, to him, anything that kids are not supposed to do. So it meant "odd" or "unusual," or "queer," in one sense; but it also meant anything that was too much like what a goody-goody would do. Doing homework ahead of time and turning it in early was gay; wearing one's Cub Scout uniform to school was gay; not having seen PG-13 movies at age ten was gay.* Nowhere in his description was sex mentioned at all. When his mother explained what *gay* meant in the sense of sexual preference, Peter knew what she meant, but he expressed surprise at her stupidity for thinking he was talking about sex. He looked at her with compassion and said, "Mom, I don't know anyone who does that; I'm too young."

Later, of course, when sex becomes more interesting as they approach puberty, kids learn that nerds are asexual and gays are homosexual. Earlier on, nerds and gays are leftover babies; that is, the terms refer to something very negative about a child's relationship with adults. How this turns into intelligence, physical repulsiveness, or *Star Trek* fandom is a complicated story (see below). But part of the complication, once again, is the total illogic of the nerd stereotype. For kids, nerds start out, conceptually, as people who do things primarily to please adults: They do well in school; they do practical things that look ridiculous (like wear pocket protectors or fanny packs) as adults always urge kids to do. We might notice

---

*My college students will frequently label the practical things their professors do, like using a tray in the cafeteria or wearing their reading glasses around their necks, as "gay."

that part of the definition for younger kids is that nerds are kids who are too attached to adults and too willingly pleasing. So why then does the stereotype include being inattentive to one's hygiene? Remember, on the geek T-shirt self-test, one of the items is "Deodorant is as foreign a concept as toothpaste or mouthwash." Where did that come from? All kids know that those kids who like to please adults—who do well in school and wear things like fanny packs—are also well cared for: Their teeth are always squeaky clean, because their mommies want them to brush their teeth. Being personally unclean, unwashed, or smelly is a symptom of parental neglect, and every schoolkid knows this. So in order to learn the full definition of *nerd*, they have to wrap their minds around another false premise: that kids who succeed in pleasing adults are neglected by those same adults. No wonder it takes so much indoctrination to get the concept across.

We will return to a discussion about where all these bizarre premises come from, but for now, we might observe that this early part of the "nerd" concept—the part that defines nerds as kids who are interested in pleasing adults—is something that parents should be concerned about. Parents who talk about nerds or endorse their children's contempt for nerds are sowing dragon's teeth: In effect, they are saying to their kids, "I have contempt for children who are close to their parents or who are interested in pleasing their parents." Needless to say, it is a message to one's children that bears some reexamination, because it is one short step from that to "In order for you not to be ridiculed by me, you must defy me." Uh-oh, bad adolescence dead ahead.

By the time he was twelve, Peter was almost fully indoctrinated. When I asked him then about nerds, he gave me the
full story: how nerds wear Coke-bottle glasses (this from a
child who, I would wager, has never seen a glass Coke bottle),
collared shirts with pocket protectors, and very short shorts
with knee socks and dress shoes. (For some reason, these are
Oktoberfest nerds.) They look ridiculous. They are "studious
but not in a good way." I ask him what he means. "They're
extremely studious, and they're suck-ups. Like they always
want the teacher to think they're smart. And they are smart.
But they always have to make sure the teacher knows it." And,
he goes on, "they don't have too many friends."

Peter's description of the prototypical nerd is noteworthy for
another characteristic: This nerd is a boy. When I ask him if
nerds can be girls, he thinks long and hard. "I guess so," he says,
"but they're usually not." How come? "I don't know. Girls don't
get called nerds, even when they act like nerds. I just think
nerds are always boys." Later, in high school, the concept "girl
nerd" comes into play, but by then it has already become, for
most kids, more elastic and differentiated. The fact that kids
use the modifier "girl" in the term "girl nerds" implies that it is
necessary to distinguish these girls from the default definition
of "nerd," which is always male. Kids who have the full stereotype in mind can't answer the question why nerds are always
male, any more than they could answer the question "Why do
preppies wear plaid?" It just is so; it is a stereotype presented to
kids by a culture that defines nerds as overwhelmingly male.[*]

---

[*]As we shall see, a large part of this story has to with American history and
the proper role of schooling in the development of the prototypical American

Peter, at twelve, knows the "right" gender for nerds. He also knows about sex, but he leaves sex itself out of the nerd definition. It still takes a little longer to get that part down. Rennie, at age sixteen, could fill him in on the rest. He is definitely postclique, in his way: He is friends with everyone in his small school, and, as a victim of severe childhood teasing, he never expresses contempt for anyone at school (except teachers). He makes a casual reference to nerds, so I ask him, what does he mean by that? "Oh, you know," he says. "Well, maybe I do," I say, "but you know me, always asking questions. What do you mean by 'nerd'?" A nerd, he tells me simply, is "smart, and they always get A's in school. But they're ugly, and they never, never get laid, 'cause no self-respecting girl would ever sleep with one of them. And they wear pocket protectors and stuff." He goes on, looking visibly embarrassed. "I like nerds, I really do. It's cool to talk to them, especially the ones who know everything about *The Lord of the Rings*. That's cool. I have friends who are really nerdy." Then he gets more obviously upset. "I don't want to talk about this any more." "Okay. Do you know how come?" "Well, you wear glasses and all . . . I mean, I don't want you to think I'm calling you a nerd." "Why not?" "Nobody wants to be called a nerd, right?"

I could go on and on with him about this, but of course he has other things on his mind. And he has already given me his (obvious, to him) insight about why it's so hard for me, or anyone like me, to talk to kids about nerds. A studious grown-up with glasses is already pretty nerdy, and, even though some of

man. Nerds and geeks are male in large part because they are extensions of nineteenth-century stereotypes of what men were supposed to be.

Rennie's best friends are nerds, he still doesn't want to insult me by calling me one. Does this sound familiar? It's the time-honored quandary of prejudice among friends: "Some of my best friends are _____s, but I really like you, so I would never dream of calling you a _____, even though you are one, *because it's a gross insult.*"

And so it remains. For adults, the term becomes something funny or hip or ironic. Young adult urban hipsters embrace nerd/geek stereotypes and costumes because this is a way of distancing themselves from mainstream America. But urban hipsters are not mainstream America. In this way, "geek chic" is like "man purses" and other manifestations of metrosexual fashion: hipsters embrace a stereotype-bending fashion statement as if to say, "Look how far beyond all that I really am." But man purses never caught on outside a few big cities, and "geek chic" has a similar problem. Geek might be chic in Greenpoint, Brooklyn, but it is not chic in Des Moines, or Dayton, or, to my knowledge, Wichita.

For genuine grown-up adults, it's a term we can all use and laugh about, about how silly we were when it might have meant something to us. And we can pretend that, as an insult, it has lost all its power, because we're all so grown-up and sophisticated now . . . until it gets used on us. Marie, a high-powered professional in her thirties, tells me of visiting her local bar after work in the big city. She takes a book with her; if she sees someone she knows, she'll schmooze with them, but if not, she might sit at the bar and read until someone comes in. The bartender is a friendly woman whom Marie has known for years. But one night, the bartender says to her, with a little edge of derision, "Got your book again?" Marie laughs, and says,

"Something wrong with that?" The bartender says, "Honey, there's nothing wrong with you. We all think you're great. You're our pet nerd." Oh, okay. Gee, thanks. Marie laughs, and feels terrible, considering the world of condescension she has brought down on herself by bringing a book to a bar.

She survived, of course. Nerds mostly survive being insulted, except those few who become suicidal in junior high school because they can't stand being vilified any longer. I have worked with such kids, so I know the issues. For example, my twelve-year-old patient Ellie was hospitalized briefly after taking an overdose of Tylenol. The reason? Her seventh-grade girlfriends were particularly vicious about her bookishness, and she slowly lost one friend after another as they decided she was too nerdy for words. When her last friend abandoned her, explaining (with what passes for compassion among seventh-graders) that she still liked her, but could not be seen with her or speak with her at school because Ellie was so nerdy that her friend's own reputation was in danger, Ellie had had enough. She took what she thought was a lethal overdose of Tylenol, and we spent the better part of a year working together to get her past it. She eventually went to an independent school, where she found a whole bunch of nerds and geeks awaiting her "like Christmas in September," as she put it in her letter. So we can say truthfully that *most* nerds survive being insulted and abandoned and all the other things that happen to them along the way.

And most nerds are not like Ellie. It is not my intention, in writing this book, to propose that no one should ever have to feel bad about anything, or that routine insults should be outlawed through legislation, or that everyday prejudice should be considered on the same level as crimes against humanity. History has taught us that everyday prejudice *can* be a precursor to crimes against humanity, but I am not proposing here that antinerd jokes, as hurtful as they are, are the first signs of some impending antinerd pogrom. Indeed, antinerd and antigeek prejudices are fascinating precisely because they are tolerated: They are not underground, so they are in many ways more easily observable than older, less tolerated but still virulent prejudices. Antinerd and antigeek prejudices are tolerated because they are seen as harmless, but they are not. They are bad for children, and they might be bad for our society as a whole, because they are recent incarnations of a very old American disease: anti-intellectualism. And anti-intellectualism, as I will argue, is very bad for children and even worse for our society as a whole.

2.

MATH SCORES AND ECONOMIC ILLS

· OR ·

WHY YOU NEED TO GO TO INDIA TO FIND AN ENGINEER

Here's another quick self-test, but this test has only one question: Since nerds and geeks are so repulsive, why would you want to be one? Or, to put it another way, if you were a nerdy kid just learning the nerd/geek stereotype and you just saw your first "Are you a geek?" T-shirt, why wouldn't you do something about it?

Let's assume, for the moment, that becoming a nerd involves some element of choice. Now, if nerdiness is a disease or a psychopathological condition, if it is some subclinical version, or *forme fruste*, of Asperger's syndrome, then this assumption must be wrong. If there is some genetic basis for nerdiness or geekiness, of course, there is nothing one can do to affect one's fate. But even on the face of it, it seems unlikely that "being" a nerd is completely beyond one's own volition; there are many other inborn behavioral programs—for example, the human proclivity to enjoy and consume sweets—that can be overcome with a little willpower. But even if there were some inborn compulsion to be nerdy, "seeming" to be a nerd must be voluntary; no kid is required to play video games for hours at a stretch, or to learn Elvish for that matter. So, to rephrase the question: Since nerds and geeks are reportedly so repulsive, why would any kid want to appear to be one?

As kids develop the nerd stereotype, some of them do, in fact, make such conscious antinerd choices. Kids who do wear glasses can get contacts, and many of them beg to do so. Kids who do love magic cards don't have to broadcast the fact that they spend their weekend afternoons at magic tournaments; they can do it in secret and conceal their magic cards from many or most of their classmates. Some of the things that get kids labeled as "nerdy" become secret vices, in the same way that fourth- or fifth-grade girls who are shamed by their classmates for playing with dolls will still play with them in secret or with a very few trusted friends. When kids learn how bad it is to be a nerd, nerdiness can go underground, and for many kids it does. But then there's the little problem of math and science. Math and science classes happen in school, in the public sphere. How can a nerd hide in plain sight?

We already know that math and science are for nerds, right? The nerd self-test on the back of the "Deluxe NERD Glasses" box tells us this very clearly: Question 3 asks, "Was your SAT math score 600 or more?" and question 30 asks, "Have you ever told a joke about chemistry or physics?" Clearly, a big part of membership in this vilified group involves being interested and doing well in math and science. Examples of this dynamic in popular culture abound. Listen to George O'Malley, cuddly doctor on the hit TV show *Grey's Anatomy*, trying to cheer up his teenage patient: "In high school, I was secretary *and* treasurer of the Dungeons and Dragons Club. I was also a mathlete . . . and I won the blue ribbon in biology club . . . best fetal pig dissection. And let me tell you, *that* had the girls knockin' down my door. . . ." It is self-evident that George was a miserable social failure because of his . . . what? His interest in math . . . or was it the biology club? His teenage patient smiles, feeling consoled; she might be a misfit but not as much as Dr. O'Malley. But to return to our question, why would you publicly participate in something that will get you labeled as a nerd if you can choose not to? For many kids, the answer is, you don't. You don't present yourself to the public as a George O'Malley. You choose not to take math classes. You choose not to do well in math. In order not to be labeled a nerd, you do not do well what those repulsive nerds do so well.

SMART KIDS, FOOLISH CHOICES

But to understand this, we have to start at the other end, that is, at the result of nerd/geek stereotypes, and the choices kids make to avoid them. Let's start with one possible result and work backward. One *possible* end result of the choices of seventh-graders is a phenomenon well known in higher-education circles: the shortage of native-born science and engineering students. The engineering shortage first made national headlines in the late 1990s, when it became apparent that the number of Ph.D.'s awarded in science and engineering was declining after several years of robust growth. Since then, policy makers in higher education and government have tried to understand the science and engineering shortage. First, does it exist and, more important, if so, what to do about it? A RAND Corporation study published in 2003 discussed the shortage not in absolute terms but in relative terms: The United States appears to be losing ground *relative to other industrialized nations* in the awarding of Ph.D.'s in science and engineering. For example, the RAND study showed that in 1980 23 percent of all science and engineering Ph.D.'s awarded in the United States went to foreign citizens; by 1994, this figure had risen to 42 percent. Even with the correction in this figure occasioned by the events of September 2001 (with concomitant restrictions on study in the United States by foreign nationals), this figure is still of concern. The RAND study also showed that the probability that a young adult would earn a four-year degree in science and engineering rose markedly between 1975 and 1999 in other developed countries, including England, Canada, France, Italy, Germany, and Japan, while the rise in the United States has been modest at best. The RAND study concluded that the United States is indeed falling behind our competitor nations in awarding science and engineering degrees. More recent data confirms this trend. The 2009 National Science Foundation survey of earned doctorates showed that students on temporary visas earned 57 percent of all earned doctorates in engineering and 45 percent of all earned doctorates in physical sciences in 2008. Although the number of foreign-born students reporting plans to stay in the United States upon completion of their studies also increased, it is far from clear that more stringent immigration regulations will allow those plans to come to fruition.

The RAND study suggested remedies for this social problem, and, being the good economists that they are, they suggested remedies that followed rational models of economic choice. Young people making career choices need to be convinced that they can make good money in science and engineering fields, as compared with medicine, law, or business. Rational economic models would suggest, of course, that a shortage in scientists and engineers would translate into higher demand, and therefore, eventually, higher compensation; the market economy should take care of the problem in time. But this presumes that young people's career choices are based on rational factors and, furthermore, that they are equally capable and prepared for choosing among science, law, and business at the time of making career decisions. Of course, this is not the case. Young people who are not science or math majors in college cannot enter Ph.D. programs in science or math; and young people who enter college far behind their foreign-born competitors in science and math achievement are less likely to choose math or science as a major in college. The model of career choice for scientists and engineers is not the same as that for lawyers—any smart, motivated English major can go to law school if his or her grades and LSATs are good enough—but choosing to be a scientist or engineer may be more like choosing to be a performing musician: You need to start a lot earlier than college in order to succeed.

And other research, which has also been the focus of national concern, suggests that American kids don't start anywhere near early enough when it comes to science and math education. By now, we are all familiar with these alarming trends: American kids do not measure up to their foreign competitors in math achievement in high school. In recent memory, this first made national headlines with the publication in 1983 of the final report of the National Commission on Excellence in Education. The report, titled "A Nation at Risk," warned of a "rising tide of mediocrity" in educational achievement. Educators and legislators across the country hastened to respond and promised reform. Indeed, by 1990, President George H. W. Bush and all the state governors had adopted a program of educational goals, including one goal in particular for math and science: "By the year 2000, United States students will be the first in the world in mathematics and science achievement."

Are we there yet? Nope. Are we even close? Nope again. And we don't look like we're getting there anytime soon. In 2003, the nation was shocked—well, sort of shocked—to read that, far from being at the top of the heap, we're still much closer to the bottom. The Program for International Student Assessment is an educational-achievement survey sponsored by the Organisation for Economic Co-operation and Development that looks at the educational achievements of fifteen-year-olds in thirty countries of the developed world. In the 2003 results, the United States ranked twenty-fourth out of twenty-nine countries surveyed. (Great Britain was left out, for not having tested enough students.) In 2006, the most recent year for which PISA data are available, U.S. fifteen-year-olds ranked twenty-first out of thirty industrialized countries in science literacy and twenty-fifth out of thirty in math literacy. Another prestigious achievement survey, the Trends in International Mathematics and Science Study (TIMSS), tests younger children, but the results for U.S. students are still not encouraging. In 2003, U.S. fourth-graders were outperformed by students in eleven other countries in math and five other countries in science testing. U.S. eighth-graders in 2003 were outperformed by students in fourteen other countries in math and eight other countries in science. In 2007, the most recent year for which TIMSS data are available, U.S. fourth-graders were outperformed by students in ten other countries in math and seven other countries in science; U.S. eighth-graders were outperformed by eight other countries in math and ten other countries in science. We weren't the worst, but sixteen years after declaring the "best in the world" as a national educational goal, we just aren't making the grade.

The news here is not all bad; there are some data suggesting that we are inching along in the project of improving math scores. American math-achievement cheerleaders can point to the National Assessment of Educational Progress—sometimes called the "Nation's Report Card"—to show some evidence of progress. But these hopeful data are also instructive about the locus of the problem, what we might term the "problem of the recalcitrant middle." On scores with a range from 0 to 500, average math NAEP scores for fourth-graders have gone up 25 points from 1990 to 2005, with three of those points accruing in the years 2003–2005. In the same period, however, average math NAEP scores for eighth-graders have gone up 16 points, but from 2003 to 2005 they have risen a measly 1 point. In my home state of Massachusetts, the data are the same: Intensive efforts to improve math scores for elementary school kids have demonstrated some positive results, while math scores in eighth grade remain mired somewhere between "dunce" and "clueless."

So when it comes to science and math achievement, we have a lot to explain. It is hardly surprising that there are fewer and fewer American kids choosing science and math majors in college and postcollege degree programs; compared with kids in other countries, American kids don't have the backgrounds to support the interest, and certainly not the success, in these fields. But why, after years of investment in raising math scores, are American kids still doing so poorly compared with their peers in the rest of the world? And why, even when improvement is seen in elementary school, does it tail off in middle school?

Policy makers in education and government are full of answers for these questions, but, as you might expect, their answers strongly suggest remedies that can be implemented by policy makers. Much of the NAEP literature, for example, is frankly political: If we had more standardization and more high-stakes testing—that is, more "accountability"—kids would do better in math and science (and reading, for that matter). The American tradition of local control of education is cited by national and international observers as a speed bump, if not a genuine roadblock, on the highway to math achievement. Many of the countries on the top of the math heap have standardized and centralized math curricula and, more important, many more required math courses. It does not take a rocket scientist, or a math geek, to figure out that kids who have taken more, and therefore more advanced, math courses do better on standardized tests of math achievement and that this effect increases as one progresses in high school. Finland, for example, has one standard curriculum for both math and science for the entire country, and since there is little or no ability grouping, everyone is required to learn the same amount of math. To Finns, our national patchwork of math standards must seem quaint at best—another relic of our decentralized agrarian past. And speaking of our agrarian past, let's not forget another explanation for greater math achievement scores, especially in Asia: The school year there is a whole month longer. So why should we be surprised their kids know more?

Other culprits in the Math Achievement Finger-Pointing Hall of Fame are familiar enough to veterans of the "culture wars" of the last decade. There are, believe it or not, "math wars" going on, between traditionalists who emphasize a style of math teaching based on brute-force memorization of math facts and learning by rote and advocates of "fuzzy math," who emphasize teaching math in real-world contexts and teaching math concepts in student-centered and approachable formats. These math wars are almost identical to the reading wars of the last decades: Should we teach reading using phonics or use the "whole language" approach? And the math wars have yielded about as much as the reading wars have: a great deal of research, much of it contradictory, but all of it in service of an underlying "culture wars" paradigm. According to this paradigm, our kids' problems with math are part of a broader lack of discipline encouraged by a degenerate culture—or not, depending on which side of the culture wars you're on.

Policy makers are, of course, much less likely to embrace cultural explanations. After all, changing the "culture" is something policy makers like to prescribe for others (Daniel Patrick Moynihan's famous nostrums on the "culture of poverty" being but one example), but changing a culture is apparently a lot less appetizing when it comes to empowered middle- and upper-middle-class Americans. It seems plausible, at least, to suggest one cultural factor that might explain both the comparatively poor math achievement of American kids and the problem of the "recalcitrant middle"—why improving test scores gets so much harder in middle school.

PRETTY GIRLS AND PRETTY BOYS

It's the sex, stupid. Well, not real intercourse, but it's the puberty and the promise of sexual intercourse. There is one thing middle school kids all have in common, and it's not algebra. All middle school kids are developing sexual desires, and they are asking themselves the same question: When is *it* going to happen to me? They might be asking it quietly or loudly. Some are so anxious about the question that they seek to answer it by making *it* happen all too quickly; others are content (if you can call it that) to fantasize about the day when *it* will happen. But thinking about sex is what middle school is all about, and therefore algebra is out.

Now, please note, I am not making the argument that some educators and parents make: Kids are all so preoccupied with their "hormones" that they can't concentrate anyway, so we shouldn't even try to educate them in middle school; we'll just babysit them until they get to high school. It is difficult to educate middle school kids, but that is no excuse not to try. The idea that we can't bother to educate them because they are too preoccupied has no more weight than its historically older counterpart: that we need to keep them busy, so busy with hard schoolwork that they will have to keep their minds off their gonads. Kids in middle school can learn anything they want, if they are motivated to do so. It is one thing to be preoccupied with sex, as many middle school kids are, but it is quite another to be constantly informed that doing well in science or math will actually make you less likely to have sex, ever. This is the one big countermotivation that they learn every day they watch television: People who like science or math never get *it*. That's what they learn from "Are you a nerd?" selftests, and that's what they learn from George O'Malley on *Grey's Anatomy*. They learn that, somehow, studying math and science makes you unattractive, if not downright ugly.[*]

Of course, this is something that women have always known. Women have been told for centuries that being smarter than men will never get them a husband and that even looking smart is a turnoff for men. Contemporary teenage girls may not have heard the phrase, popular in the past among purveyors of contact lenses—"Men don't make passes at girls who wear glasses"—but they will understand the sentiment all the same. This had something to do with making sure your man never felt that you, the girl in question, were superior to him in any way. It was not inherently an association between intellectuality and ugliness. But how many of us have seen, over and over, the following iconic scene in movies, television shows, or cartoons? You know the scene. It's the one where the lady scientist or doctor, who until now has been wearing a shapeless

---

[*]Later in the series, O'Malley sheds his nerdy beginnings. He ends up sleeping with the hot blonde doctor who paid her way through medical school by being a lingerie model. But immediately afterward he fails an important medical examination, proving once again that sex actually makes you stupid (see chapter 5).

lab coat and big ugly glasses and has her hair pulled back in a severe and unattractive bun, removes her glasses and lets her hair down and takes off the lab coat and reveals herself to be . . . Pamela Anderson or Salma Hayek or Christina Aguilera. Women know all about how looking "smart" turns off a man. This is one reason many educators insist on gender-segregated science and math classes for girls, and one of the major arguments, over the years and still today, for women's colleges: Women can feel free to be excellent, especially in science and math, if there are no men around to "dumb down" for.

But now we face a dramatically different problem: Young men are becoming, culturally speaking, women, because they are now facing the same attitudes about sex and sexiness that women have always faced. Indeed, one of the biggest changes in American teen culture in the last decade or so is the dramatic change in young men's participation in beauty culture. Young men are now, for better or worse, objectified, in a sexual sense, just as much as young women. Popular media feature "hunks" and hot young men who must meet rigid standards of sexual attractiveness just as young women have always done. To get a sense of this, one might watch several old beach-party movies, the ones with Frankie Avalon and Annette Funicello, and compare them with the sensibility on display in MTV's Spring Break TV specials every year. The disparities in the treatment of men as sex objects are enormous: In the old days, cute guys were cute but not that cute, and even not-cute guys got to date cute girls. Now, as MTV demonstrates, there is an aristocracy of the body that affects men as much as women: Only the hottest bodies are allowed to pair off, and less-than-hot bodies can only aspire to less-than-hot bodies of the opposite sex. While some women might see this treatment of young men as just deserts for centuries of female objectification, it is not exactly what one might wish for in terms of gender equality.

For more evidence of the new condition of young men, ask any mental-health professional who treats adolescents. They will tell you all about the new body-image problems of young male patients: steroid abuse, injuries from excessive weight lifting or self-starving, and all the other distortions of body image and self-esteem traditionally seen only in anorexic teenage girls. The syndrome is now familiar enough to have its own name: In 2000 Harvard psychiatrist Harrison Pope coined the term "Adonis Complex" in a book on the subject. He points to a number of cultural changes that contribute to the male version of anorexia, mostly changing media stereotypes. One example Pope offers is G.I. Joe. In 1964 a G.I. Joe figure would have had, had he been an adult male, biceps twelve inches in diameter. In 2000, a G.I. Joe figure blown up to life size would have had biceps twenty-seven inches in diameter, or essentially as big as his twenty-seven-inch waist. Playthings for boys now present body images just as unattainable as those of Barbie dolls have always been, and boys are responding the way girls have for years: with increasingly self-destructive efforts to look like the new G.I. Joe. So far, the Adonis Complex appears to be largely an American disease, but we can expect that it will travel along with the American media that spawns it. As anthropologists and epidemiologists have documented, the incidence of anorexia nervosa rises in the developing world in direct proportion to exposure to American media culture. So why should "male anorexia" be any different?

To me, this looks like a smoking gun. On one side, we have a well-documented decline in achievement and interest in math and science in America that appears to be extraordinarily resistant to change, especially at the middle school level. On the other side, we have a cultural stereotype that rigidly enforces a separation between interest in math and science and sexual attractiveness: Kids learn early and often that nerds are ugly sexual failures. And we have a teen culture that has taken the traditional emphasis on beauty-above-all-else it has imposed on young women and applied it just as rigidly to young men. So should we be surprised that middle school kids, both boys and girls, don't want to study math? They do grow out of their crude stereotypes about nerds and geeks, and eventually learn that you really can know a lot about math *and* get laid, so we don't take the stereotypes all that seriously. But guess what? By the time they outgrow the stereotypes, they're several years behind their foreign counterparts in math studies, and they can't catch up.

SOCIAL SHAME AND MATH ACHIEVEMENT

What might we need to prove this hypothesis? Several lines of inquiry might point us in the direction of a more definitive proof, including educational research, cross-cultural studies, and (my favorite) talking to kids themselves.

The educational research seems like it might be simple enough. One could design a study that assesses kids' "nerd anxiety," or strength of nerd prejudice, and then assess their interests or achievements in math or science. Have studies like this been done? Nope. The ERIC (Educational Resources Information Clearinghouse) database, the foundational tool for educational research, advertises itself as having access to 1.3 million citations of educational research, but when you type in the search term "nerd," you get twenty-five citations, and three of them are different versions of the same paper on Asian-American kids and the nerd identity. The papers are interesting and useful, but they all address the problem of nerd labeling or how the labels affect kids who are already labeled as nerds. There appears to be no interest in the effects of nerd stereotyping on nonnerds, or any formal test of the not-particularly-surprising-or-counterintuitive hypothesis outlined above: that, in a hypersexualized culture, when kids learn that nerds are (a) good at science and math and (b) creepy and unsexy, they might lose interest in science and math.

The one study that comes close is a cross-cultural one done in Germany of math achievement and prejudice toward nerds. The study, published in 2004 in the online edition of *Ongoing Themes in Psychology and Culture*, investigated the German word *Streber,* an idiomatic term that the authors note is difficult to translate but is located somewhere between "nerd" and "teacher's pet": a student who is enthusiastic, eager to please the teacher, and therefore appears to be opportunistic to his fellow students. (Note that although the authors state that "nerd" is the best translation, they do not emphasize the sexually unappealing aspect of the nerddom.) The study looked at fourteen-year-old students in Germany, Canada, and Israel, and found that anxiety about being labeled a *Streber* (or, in Canada, a nerd; in Israel, a *hnun*) was negatively correlated with math achievement: The more worried kids were about the labeling, the worse their grades . . . except in Israel, where the correlation did not exist. So, what research evidence does exist suggests that fear of social rejection actually does have some effect on achievement, at least in Germany and Canada.[*]

There are a few more recent studies regarding the effect of nerd prejudices on young people's achievement. One was done in Australia, where researchers are trying to investigate systematically why more young women do not take up math as a career. And one study done in England by Heather Mendick and reported in *ScienceDaily* in 2008 shows that (surprise, surprise) knowledge of and concern about the nerd stereotype does affect young people's achievement in math and their willingness to pursue math as a career. But apparently, one has to go abroad to find the interest in this kind of systematic research: once again, the stereotype appears to be so ingrained in own our culture that systematic investigation does not occur to the educational researcher.

The cross-cultural nature of the German study suggests our second line of inquiry: nerddom around the globe. If there are more kids doing better in math and science in other parts of the world, does this mean that the cultures involved have less virulent nerd stereotypes? This is difficult to assess, because kids all over the world now have access to American media, and the products that kids want most from the States are music

---

[*]This hypothesis is my gift to all you doctoral students in education desperately searching for a dissertation topic. Have fun!

and television (and blue jeans). So finding pure indigenous cultures of contemporary teenagers who have not been exposed to the concepts "nerd" and "geek" is pretty difficult. The good news here, from the point of view of American competitiveness, is that since our media culture is one of our most reliable exports, even as we speak, kids in Latvia and Burma and Micronesia are learning that if you're doing well in math and science, you won't be getting *it* anytime soon. So we might see the competitive advantages of foreigners leveling off any day now.

But while we wait, what about nerds around the world? The German study cited above points out how difficult it is to translate slang terms of adolescence from one place to another. But more important, what happens when you ask grown-ups? Anthropologic research is pretty much absent on the subject, but asking individuals tells another story.

Here's a story from Kumar, a blogger and e-friend I met while researching this book. Kumar grew up in India, and has lived and worked in the West, where he worked in computer technology. I asked Kumar, "Are there nerds and geeks in India?" and this was his reply:

My perspective on nerd/geek stereotypes in India has changed a bit from what I have seen during my 'growing up' years in India and then during my annual visits to India for the past seven years. The change in my perception can be correlated to the changes in the Indian cultural milieu due to globalization, and if I may use the overused term, the 'Americanization' of India.

Firstly, a brief account of the earlier days. Typically, the smart boys in the class (the studious people) were respected and parents used to urge their kids to emulate the top rankers in school. Being good at studies would ensure a good stream (Maths, Physics, Chemistry, Biology) in pre-university courses and then the Holy Grail of all programs in college, Engineering/Medicine. Even the kids who were good at sports used to leave sports and focus on studies once they got admission to a prestigious college of engineering through sports quotas.

Of course, some of us used to read about nerds/geeks in American schools, mainly in fiction and through some movies (like Revenge of the Nerds). In Indian films and stories read by students, the male/female leads would always stand out in terms of both physical attributes as well as mental powers. The only 'secular' differentiation one could see among the students was that of urban sophisticate versus country hick.

Being good at studies was/is definitely a plus factor. If the student was good at sports alone and bad at studies, it was a negative factor. Being good at sports (a jock) was tolerated only when the student scored at least average marks in studies.

However, in the past 10 years or so, the Indian socio-cultural setup has seen huge changes. New age careers have come up, and along with American entertainment, a lot of American ideas about college life and the associated stereotypes have set in. Most people are aware of the nerd/geek stereotype, but the negative connotation is not as strong as it is in the US. Possible reason: Some of the most successful people of Indian origin in the US are geeks. And the latest god in the Indian pantheon is a geek (Bill Gates). I may be over emphasizing the 'Gates' point, but believe me, for the average Indian, what counts is success in the US, and Gates, being the richest person in the world and being seen as some one who has done it with such consummate ease, is the role model and symbolizes America for many Indians.

But in most cases, after graduation, if a person has a good software job and is likely to settle down in the US or in an Indian metro with a very high salary, the guy can get a choice, trophy bride through arranged marriage. The very girls who would have dated the handsome, smart guys at college, would happily agree to marry a boy suggested by their parents, a boy who is a techie/MBA type. The geeks get the 'cream' among the girls.

If you talk to young people across the world, they tell a story similar to Kumar's. In Western Europe, there are concepts somewhat similar to nerdiness in some places but not in others. Spain, for example, seems to have known nothing of nerds until recent exposure to American movies and television. Asia seems to have very little acquaintance with the concept: The notion that there might be something wrong with doing well in school is laughable to Asian parents and kids, especially those who have not been exposed to Western media. It is difficult to generalize from individual anecdotes, but we might begin by noting that nerddom is far from universal.

There are no comparative anthropological studies of the concepts "nerd" and "geek", but there are anthropologists with opinions. I asked my colleague Mirka Prazak, a professor of anthropology at Bennington College, to weigh in on the subject, and she did what she always does: She went to her worldwide network of informants. Her summary? "The nerd/geek stereotype is a luxury. Some cultures have their versions; others do not. But it seems to me that the likelihood of having such a stereotype is inversely related to how long a culture has been literate. In places where many adults are still struggling to become literate or when near-universal literacy has been achieved within living memory, 'wise ones' are always venerated, not punished. It's only in cultures where everyone can read and go to school that such stereotypes can even begin to take root. Otherwise, the costs are too high."

NERDS AND MATH: THE INSIDE STORY

So when you talk to real kids about nerds and math or nerds and science, what do they tell you? It depends on whom and how you ask. If you start by talking about nerds and nerdiness, kids won't even dream of talking openly about whether or not they like math or do well in math, but if you start the conversation with the topic of math, you can learn a lot anyway. Kids who do well in math and like it, especially in middle school, don't think much about it. But kids who don't like math always bring up nerdiness as a reason for their disenchantment.

Peter, whom we met in the previous chapter, is a bright kid who at thirteen described himself as "not a math kind of guy." What does that mean? "Well, I could be better at it, but I'm just not interested." What kind of kid is interested in math?

"People who drool." Huh? "There's this kid in my class who's a math genius, but he grosses everyone out because he drools all the time." Is there anyone else in your class who's good at math but who doesn't drool? "I suppose . . . but they don't really advertise it." His older brother Angelo, at sixteen, had been evaluated at age ten as being "gifted" in math. When speaking with him at sixteen, he describes himself as "not all that good in math," and indeed he is still in advanced classes but is getting straight C's. What's up? "I don't know. It's just like so corporate to be good at math." Corporate? "Like all those kids want to go to Princeton and then go on to Wall Street. That's who's good at math." "I remember when you were good at math," I say. He smiles sheepishly. "I was such a dork then. I can't believe how dorky I was."

It is impossible to know, without reverting to waterboarding, which comes first for these brothers, the difficulties with math or the icky stereotypes of who is a "math person." Certainly the nerd stereotype can be compensatory: If a kid wants to be good at math and isn't, he can tell himself that only creepy nerds are good at math, and who wants to be one of those anyway? It is not necessarily the stereotype that comes first, *causing* the disinterest in kids with normal or above-normal math abilities, but the stereotype is there, and it certainly works against kids' changing course: Once they decide they are "not a math person," they have a ready-made, very powerful reason for not trying to become a "math person."

Frank, at twenty, is a sophomore at a prestigious eastern liberal arts college, the kind of place parents would commit murder to get their kids into. And Frank actually wants to be a science major. He is also a handsome, self-confident ladies' man who has never had any trouble getting girls. "My friends make fun of me for wanting to major in biology," he says. What do they major in? "Film, or English. History. Not science." Do you care? "Sometimes. When we go to a party, they tell me not to mention I might be a bio major." Do you listen to them? "Not really. But it pisses me off. What happens when I am a bio major? Am I gonna sink into social oblivion?" Frank is old enough to know better, but that's the point: He has made it past the worst years for nerd stereotyping, with his interest in science intact. And even for him, it's still a liability.

The big story that Frank and Peter and Angelo have to tell is one about growing up. These kids, and the thousands or millions of others like them who feel the same way, know by the time they're juniors in high school that the nerd stereotype is silly and that it's no excuse for not pursuing what you like. But by then, it's too late: Foundations of math education start years earlier. Kids are not stupid: A recent study from the Michigan Department of Education documented that 48 percent of all post–high school kids surveyed said they wished they had taken more advanced math classes in high school. But they didn't. And their story demonstrates the head-on collision between a complex stereotype like the nerd/geek story and the primitive black-and-white thinking of late childhood and early adolescence. We, the grown-ups who write the nerd self-tests and produce TV shows like *The Big Bang Theory*, know it's all a joke, *but our kids don't*. So, my friend, go to India if you want to hire an engineer—by now, you might have to go to rural India or until-very-recently-rural India—but that's where those engineering kids are.

Why do Americans keep telling this particular joke?

Indeed, why is this stereotype so taken for granted by American educational researchers that it seems beyond investigation? The big reason is found in American history. We have a long tradition of being suspicious of intellectual achievement, a tradition almost as old as our nation. So whom do we have to thank for our dependence on foreign-born scientists and engineers? Unlikely culprits but culprits all the same: Washington Irving and Ralph Waldo Emerson.

3.

OLD THEMES
AND NEW TWISTS

· OR ·

WHY ICHABOD CRANE WILL
NEVER GET LAID

He was a native of Connecticut, a State which supplies the
Union with pioneers for the mind as well as for the forest,
and sends forth yearly its legions of frontier woodmen and
country schoolmasters. The cognomen of Crane was not
inapplicable to his person. He was tall, but exceedingly lank,
with narrow shoulders, long arms and legs, hands that dan-
gled a mile out of his sleeves, feet that might have served for
shovels, and his whole frame most loosely hung together.
His head was small, and flat at top, with huge ears, large
green glassy eyes, and a long snipe nose, so that it looked
like a weathercock perched upon his spindle neck to tell
which way the wind blew. To see him striding along the pro-
file of a hill on a windy day, with his clothes bagging and flut-
tering about him, one might have mistaken him for the
genius of Famine descending upon the earth or some scare-
crow eloped from a cornfield.

If you've gone to school in the United States of America, you will probably recognize this laughable figure. Why, it's Ichabod Crane! He's the hero (of sorts) of Washington Irving's famous story "The Legend of Sleepy Hollow." Mr. Crane is the schoolmaster in the little backwater settlement on the banks of the Hudson at a time when folks could still dimly remember the parts their fathers played in the American Revolution. He is the town intellectual, since it is his job to teach the schoolboys to read, and he has actually read a few books himself. He also teaches the art of psalm-singing to make a few extra shillings. So, in his way, he represents both literature and art in Irving's story, and as his physical description shows and his actions demonstrate, he is America's first nerd.

How do we know? After all, he doesn't watch *Star Trek* or spend the afternoon playing with his magic cards. But he does spend the afternoon reading, which not too many denizens of Sleepy Hollow do. And what does he read? He reads about the supernatural: When he disappears at the end of the story, he leaves behind his own copies of "Cotton Mather's *History of Witchcraft*, a *New England Almanac*, and a book of dreams and fortune-telling." He indulges in fantasies about magic, sorcerers, and witches. He is, like Dr. George O'Malley, the secretary and treasurer of the Dungeons & Dragons Club, early-nineteenth-century version. He is also pathologically unself-conscious: He is ridiculous, but he doesn't know it. We know he doesn't know he's ridiculous, because we see him delude himself. He even allows himself to imagine that he will win the hand of Katrina Van Tassel, the prettiest and richest maiden in Sleepy Hollow.

Ichabod Crane is a nerd without the technology—a crucial

point to which we will return—but he is also a nerd because he is persecuted by a nonnerd. He is, by definition, *not* what his opposite number *is*.

> The most formidable [of Katrina's other suitors] was a burly, roaring, roystering blade of the name of Abraham—or, according to the Dutch abbreviation, Brom—Van Brunt, the hero of the country round, which rang with his feats of strength and hardihood. He was broad shouldered and double-jointed, with short curly black hair and a bluff but not unpleasant countenance, having a mingled air of fun and arrogance. From his Herculean frame and great powers of limb, he had received the nickname *Brom Bones*, by which he was universally known. He was famed for great knowledge and skill in horsemanship, being as dextrous on horseback as a Tartar. . . . He was always ready for either a fight or a frolic, but had more mischief than ill-will in his composition; and with all his overbearing roughness there was a strong dash of waggish good-humour at bottom.

Poor Ichabod never has a chance. Brom Bones gets the girl, but those who have not read the story recently might not remember that he does not get the girl by default. He drives Ichabod out of town by scaring him out of his wits, but this happens only *after* Ichabod has been rejected by the lovely Katrina Van Tassel; it is strongly suggested in the story that Ichabod's dejection after having been dumped contributes to his unconquerable terror when he sees the Headless Horseman. It is very clear that Katrina does not want Ichabod, the captain of the Geek Squad; she wants, and eventually gets,

Brom Bones, the captain of the football team. And after Ichabod disappears mysteriously, everyone is so glad to be rid of
him that learning itself suffers. His landlord, Hans Van Ripper,
consigns Ichabod's books and his poor attempts at poetry to
the flames, and "from that time forward determined to send
his children no more to school, observing that he never knew
any good come of this same reading and writing."

This wonderful story was written in 1819 and published in
The Sketch Book of Geoffrey Crayon, Gent., a literary sensation
in the United States and England that was heralded as the
beginning of a truly native American Literature, with a capital L.
One can see, just from reading this one story, why the book
caught on in both places, an unlikely feat given the historical
animosity between Britain and its former colony. The irony is
just ironic enough for the book to rest comfortably between
the two continents: The small-mindedness and superstition of
the Dutch burghers is gently mocked, but Ichabod Crane is
mocked even more. In fact, it is not really a story about a competition between two people, Brom and Ichabod, but one
about three competing forces: the American "intellectual," who
is undone by his interest in old-fashioned European superstition; the superstitious and ignorant Dutch settlers, who with
their funny names and old-country ways resemble Europeans
more than they do Americans; and finally the wily, tough hero
who ignores superstition, but uses it to his advantage, Brom
Bones, the real American. Irving manages to mock European
superstition and American intellectual pretensions at the same
time, but the winner is clearly a new American type: the anti-
intellectual hero.

So why do we contemporary Americans, who are so careful

about everything we let our children consume, let our children read this book? Parents in the United States object vociferously to any required reading in public schools that even hints at children having an interest in anything unhealthy, like sex or drugs; these books are way too dangerous for our children to consume. One need only consult the American Library Association's list of "challenged" books, that is, books that someone has attempted to remove from libraries or classrooms, to see the pattern of what is considered unwholesome. The list of the ten most challenged books from the decade 1990 to 2000 contains classics like *The Adventures of Huckleberry Finn, The Catcher in the Rye,* and *Of Mice and Men,* as well as current causes célèbres like *Heather Has Two Mommies* and *Daddy's Roommate* (in case you're wondering, the roommate in question is not a lovable dog).

But apparently everyone enthusiastically embraces "The Legend of Sleepy Hollow," which teaches the lesson that reading is stupid and teachers are ridiculous, unappealing, self-deluded bores. The story appears in required-reading lists for kids as young as fourth grade (in high-powered private schools) and in read-aloud formats in public school curricula all the way through elementary school. It appears in middle school required-reading lists throughout the country. It is performed as a play in elementary and middle schools, and even as a children's opera. In 1949 the Walt Disney studio produced it as an animated short feature with voice-over narration and original songs performed by no less than Bing Crosby. In the early 1980s it was recorded by the beloved folks at Rabbit Ears Radio with narration by Glenn Close; the Rabbit Ears video version appeared in 1997 (proving once again that liberal, openhearted PBS types are just as self-destructive as everybody else when it comes to contributing to the dumbing-down of American culture).

I am not a big believer in censorship, and I love "The Legend of Sleepy Hollow." It is a wonderful story for adults. For priceless satire, you can't beat the description of Ichabod imagining every one of old Van Tassel's turkeys and geese in its already cooked form. But adults don't read it in America; we give it to kids to read. It is a cherished piece of Americana, and we give it to them so they can learn something about what it means to be an American. And while kids love it for the spookiness and the ambiguity—was it really the Headless Horseman, or was it Brom Bones pretending to be the Headless Horseman?—they are also getting the message, thanks to us, that learning, and the learned, are ridiculous. After all, kids are kids; the subtleties of the messages about Europe and America are not going to be appreciated the way adults appreciate subtleties. They will identify with someone in the story, one person, and it will not be Ichabod Crane; the last thing kids want is to be seen to be goofy. So who's it gonna be?

If this story were new, I believe that parents, especially those parents who value achievement, would object. Imagine, if you will, a newly published book written by one of our ubiquitous authors of books for "young adults," about a kid who tries to do well in school but is kind of pedantic, and who in the course of the story is ridiculed and then run out of town by a juvenile delinquent. The delinquent ends up getting the girl of his dreams and a nice position in the girl's father's firm. End of story. Such a book might get published, but it wouldn't be required reading, and we even might hope that more than a few solicitous parents would object. But "The Legend of Sleepy Hollow" is so much a part of American culture that we don't really notice it. It is like background, the air we breathe. This portrait of American practicality and physicality as opposed to musty, superstitious European book-learning is our intellectual legacy. It does not seem offensive, because it is, in some powerful ways, us.

AMERICAN SCHOLARSHIP AND "THE AMERICAN SCHOLAR"

Washington Irving, after all, was not the only American promoting the denigration of intellectuals as being somehow "European." None other than the great Ralph Waldo Emerson promoted the idea of the distinct character of the American intellectual in his 1837 address "The American Scholar," delivered, ironically enough, to the Phi Beta Kappa Society at Harvard College. This address has sometimes been described as the most important academic address in American history; it was called, by no less than Oliver Wendell Holmes, "the Declaration of Independence of the American intellectual." It gives voice in the loftiest academic diction to a repeated theme in American history: that Americans are, first and foremost, men of action, not men of reflection. (A note of apology: In the following discussion I will be referring to scholars and educated men as "men," because in the time of Irving and Emerson, they were. Educating girls came later, for various reasons and with a different ideological history attached.)

Emerson's address to the Phi Beta Kappans is complicated. One might even, on close reading, say that it is tricky. Emerson was an intellectual speaking to the most intellectual assembly America had to offer at the time. But in "The American Scholar," he reinvents the intellectual as a distinctly American type: a man who thinks but, more important, who acts. In the essay, Emerson extols the virtues of the three great "teachers" for the American scholar: Nature, books, and action. Books are not given primacy, and although Emerson lauds book-learning, by the time he is done with it you wonder why anyone would want to participate.

He begins with a disquisition on the appropriate division of labor in a modern society. Professional thinkers are okay with Emerson as long as they don't think too much.

> In this distribution of functions, the scholar is the delegated intellect. In the right state, he is, *Man Thinking*. In the degenerate state, when the victim of society, he tends to become a mere thinker, or, still worse, the parrot of other men's thinking. . . . But the old oracle said, "All things have two handles: beware of the wrong one." In life, too often, the scholar errs with mankind and forfeits his privilege.

Scholars are not special, Emerson lets us know; they're just as likely as anyone else, possibly more so, to end up in the wrong. Emerson continues with man's need for schooling by Nature, Emerson's great preoccupation. The anti-intellectual implication here is still only an implication: that direct observation of Nature cannot, and should not, be tainted by the observations of people of the past. So far, so good, although he is a little squishy about how the great observers of Nature he admires (Linnaeus, Davy, and Cuvier, for example) are to communicate their brilliant observations if not via books. But it is in the section on *books* as instructors of scholars that Emerson takes a hard turn:

> Books are written on it by thinkers, not by Man Thinking; by men of talent, that is, who start wrong, who set out from accepted dogmas, not from their own sight of principles. Meek young men grow up in libraries, believing it their duty to accept the views, which Cicero, which Locke, which Bacon, have given, forgetful that Cicero, Locke, and Bacon were only young men in libraries, when they wrote these books. . . . Hence, instead of Man Thinking, we have the bookworm. Hence, the book-learned class, who value books, as such; not as related to nature and the human constitution, but as making a sort of Third Estate with the world and the soul. Hence, the restorers of readings, the emendators, the bibliomaniacs of all degrees.

Ick. Who wants to be one of those? In another sleight of hand, Cicero, Locke, and Bacon are relegated to the class of "young men in libraries," just like *we* were when *we* were scholars. The democratic ideal is paramount here: Those guys were no smarter than you or me, so don't read their books; go write your own.[*] Eventually, Emerson relents a little, and

---

[*]One can only imagine that Emerson would have been transcendentally happy in the age of blogging, when everyone can and does write his or her own book.

allows us to revere books but only when we run short of inspiration (or Inspiration, as he might have written).

> Books are for the scholar's idle times. When he can read God directly, the hour is too precious to be wasted in other men's transcripts of their readings. But when the intervals of darkness come, as come they must,—when the sun is hid, and the stars withdraw their shining,—we repair to the lamps which were kindled by their ray, to guide our steps to the East again, where the dawn is. . . . I would not be hurried by any love of system, by any exaggeration of instincts, to underrate the Book. We all know, that, as the human body can be nourished on any food, though it were boiled grass and the broth of shoes, so the human mind can be fed by any knowledge.

It seems that books are okay after all, in the way that boiled grass and shoe broth are okay as nutrition. So much for American scholarship.

Emerson gets even trickier on the subject of the character of intellectuals. The essay is bold, to be sure, and it is nothing short of insultingly bold when one imagines the context. He was speaking in an institution founded for the purpose of educating young men for the clergy and at a time when that purpose was still an important function of a Harvard education. So when he gets to the subject of the character of learned men, it was courageous, in its weird way, for him to report the common American stereotype of the time: that educated men are effeminate. Like any slimy contemporary politician, he reports the insult ostensibly to repudiate it, but the rhetorical trick is the same: He gets the slur into the record. And the slur he asserts is that scholars are so indisposed to action that they might as well be women.

> There goes in the world a notion, that the scholar should be a recluse, a valetudinarian,—as unfit for any handiwork or public labor, as a penknife for an axe. The so-called "practical men" sneer at speculative men, as if, because they speculate or *see*, they could do nothing. I have heard it said that the clergy,—who are always, more universally than any other class, the scholars of their day,—are addressed as women; that the rough, spontaneous conversation of men they do not hear, but only a mincing and diluted speech. They are often virtually disfranchised; and, indeed, there are advocates for their celibacy. As far as this is true of the studious classes, it is not just and wise.

Excuse me, Ralph. Advocates for their celibacy? He does not explain, of course, why "practical men" should join up with the pope and advocate that (presumably Protestant) preachers should not be allowed to procreate . . . or can't, because they are so attuned to the world of books that they cannot act in the world as men act. Perhaps he means that the mincing scholars are advocating for their own celibacy. But the insult is there, and as Emerson goes on to advocate for the American scholar as a man of action, he implicitly endorses the sentiment of these "practical men."

"The American Scholar" can be read in any number of ways. It is not a great oration like those of Lincoln or Martin Luther King, Jr., which are uplifting because they are unambiguous in the sentiments they express. Emerson's address is much more ambiguous. It can be read as a celebration of a new American way of learning, a prefiguration of John Dewey and all the other educational progressives of the early and middle twentieth century: Emerson might be asserting, like Dewey, the primacy of "knowing how" over "knowing that." But "The American Scholar" is tricky because it is both a celebration and a condemnation of books and of scholarship, and it went a long way in promoting and giving an intellectual stamp of approval to a divide that needed no promoting: the placement of healthy action and healthy sexuality on one side of a cultural chasm and intellectual pursuits on the other.

Indeed, the divide between the images of men of action and men of reflection had already, by the time of Emerson's address, become a standard American theme. Emerson's address might be seen as simply the frosting on a very unappealing cake. The cake, so to speak, was described elegantly and at great length by the historian Richard Hofstadter, whose classic work *Anti-intellectualism in American Life* won the Pulitzer Prize for non-fiction in 1964. Hofstadter devoted considerable space to the politics of the period of the 1820s and 1830s, that is, the period of Washington Irving and Emerson's formative years. It is a politics dominated by the decline of the educated gentlemen who led the American Revolution, the Adamses and Jeffersons, and the ascendancy of the proudly uneducated, the Andrew Jacksons and the Davy Crocketts of American politics. The political discourse of the time was unrestrained, to say the least, and the conflicts between educated aristocrats and the common man were harsh in the extreme. The attacks on Jefferson, especially, for being too learned, too philosophical, and above all, too *French*, were savage, but they were nothing compared with what was later visited on John Quincy Adams by the followers of Jackson. Hofstadter pointed out that the election of 1828 was cast as a contest between "John Quincy Adams who can write, and Andrew Jackson who can fight," and Adams was slaughtered in every region of the country except New England. The themes of the campaign could be summarized simply enough, as Hofstadter noted: "As the two sides fashioned the public images of the candidates, aristocracy was paired with sterile intellect, and democracy with native intuition and the power to act."

Hofstadter went on to document the history of anti-intellectualism in succeeding American generations, and he is unsparing when discussing intellectuals' contribution to their own marginalization. It is a complicated story, full of the romance of action on one hand and the romance of alienation on the other. But what is noteworthy for our purposes is the theme of aberrant sexuality or insufficient masculinity always lurking in the shadows, to be invoked in an indirect yet unmistakable fashion. Although Irving's Ichabod Crane is goofy, and certainly not threatening to anyone except the schoolboys he canes, the depiction of him as physically unappealing and unsuccessful in love is mild considering what was to come later. Emerson's repetition of the slur of aberrant sexuality (and, with the word "mincing," homosexuality) among "scholars" was worse, yet still it was just a hint. As Hofstadter observed, intellectuals, since the founding of our republic, have too often been characterized as bloodless, effete, unmanly, or sissified, as if Andrew Jackson were still alive and writing his own advertising copy.

What is remarkable about Emerson's and Irving's depictions

of scholars is that they predate the female dominance of American primary-school education that followed. It is unfortunate but somehow more logical (using the logic of childhood) that a rebellion of "action" against "reflection" could be played out between school-boys and female teachers: boys who sat still and learned well could always be cast as sissified, compared with their bumptious classmates, who would not be ruled by schoolmarms. But women did not outnumber men as schoolteachers until about 1860, a trend that was greatly accelerated by the Civil War. So the depiction in the young United States of scholars as effete or unmanly or "sterile" or "feminine" came long before doing well in school meant (for a boy) being subjugated by a woman. The theme of scholars or intellectuals or smart people as just plain creepy has been with us for a long time, and it is a theme that reappears in full-blown form in antinerd prejudices. Currently, nerds are not described in popular culture primarily as "gay," although sometimes the stereotype comes close. But nerds are described as sexually creepy, people who are unimaginably unattractive, people who have no hope of ever getting a date. This feature of the nerd stereotype plugs right into what it means to be an "American scholar," which is why no one ever seems to question its validity or its hilarity.

SUPERMEN AND HEROES

Given this continued refrain in American history, some of the later cultural inventions of Americans do not seem so surprising. Take Superman, for example. Superman, the quintessentially American superhero, was created in 1932 by writer Jerry Siegel and first appeared in print in Action Comics in 1938. Cultural historians and critics have been discussing the meaning of Superman for decades. His appearance during the Depression, his creation by Diaspora Jews, his relation to the urban landscape, his status as an alien with an origin in outer space—all of it has been grist for the American studies mill. Few have focused on the question that is of obvious concern to scholars of nerdity (or nerdy scholars) everywhere: Why the hell doesn't anyone recognize Clark Kent as Superman? It's a wonderful fantasy: the Man of Steel living among us, fighting for truth, justice, and the American way. But Lois Lane and Jimmy Olsen are not superpeople, they are just typical Americans, and, as typical Americans, they live their typical lives, working elbow-to-elbow with an immense, hunky coworker whose intensely physical presence is completely hidden *behind a pair of glasses?* Watching Superman movies or television shows, one can only wonder at how many times Lois Lane looks pensively at Clark Kent and says, "You know, you remind me of someone. . . ." If you were a kid like me and sometimes felt more than a little involved with the characters on the small screen, you, too, might have found yourself shouting, "Wake up, Lois! Open your eyes! He's Superman, you moron!" or something to that effect.

But Lois and Jimmy and Perry White never quite get it. How come? Because they all grew up in America, and they grew up knowing there were two kinds of people: Men of Action and Men of Reflection. And they knew that no self-respecting Man of Action would ever disguise himself as his polar opposite. It would be indecent, or psychotic, or . . . un-American. It is noteworthy in this context to recall that, when "the Superman" was invented in 1932, he was a villain whose major powers were telepathic; he began his life as an evil Man of Reflection. But he was recast in 1933 as a hero, and his powers were recast as well in his current form, primarily as a noble Man of Action. After that, it was mainly his archenemies, such as Lex Luthor, who were depicted as "evil geniuses." Superman is never presented as stupid—he does have a clever idea once in a while, as when he reverse-rotates Earth to turn back time to save the life of Lois Lane in the first of the Christopher Reeve Superman movies—but he doesn't read a lot; he doesn't really have to. It's Clark Kent who reads, and writes, and bangs away on his typewriter. Poor Clark: he is treated with the same comic condescension we all bestowed on Ichabod Crane way back when. *Plus ça change*, one might say, if one weren't afraid of appearing too French.

American history, then, demonstrates that the "Man of Action versus Man of Reflection" dichotomy so central to our national identity is the spiritual ancestor of a fair number of other weird dichotomies that still plague our cultural landscape: smart versus good, intellectual versus practical, scholar versus athlete, and nerd versus jock. None of these dichotomies really makes sense—people aren't really *required* to be one and not the other—but they all make sense if you grew up on "The Legend of Sleepy Hollow" or partook of the intellectual legacy of "The American Scholar." None of these dichotomies is particularly harmful to adults, because adults can bring a developed cognitive perspective to bear on false dichotomies and recognize the falsity or at least the serious distortions of fact. All these dichotomies are confusing to children, however, and many are harmful, because children are trying to make sense of the world and are making important decisions about their identities and their futures based on exaggerated dichotomous stereotypes. If the contemporary cultural messages about nerd/geek stereotypes are just a continuation of a long American tradition, we're all swimming upstream if we try to change them. But let's just say that from now on we'll do our kids a favor and stop teaching "The Legend of Sleepy Hollow" until they get to college. Adults will be allowed to read it, but *The Sketch Book of Geoffrey Crayon, Gent.* by Washington Irving will come with a warning sticker: "This book is for mature audiences only." What will we give our kids to read instead?

How about heroic literature? In fact, how about really good heroic literature, the kind that allows for the possibility of intelligence and physicality and, yes, sexuality to reside all in the same person? How about, for example, Homer's *Odyssey*? The *Odyssey* is a really good story. It's not a short story, composed in one form by a writer we know well, like Washington Irving. It's a long story about a complicated, multidimensional man and his life, his troubles, and his wonderful talents. The *Odyssey* is about a man who is known for his intelligence, the man who ended a war with his wits when the sheer brawn of the Greek armies had failed after ten years of fighting. It was Odysseus (Ulysses), after all, who thought up the idea of the Trojan Horse, which brought the long, bitter war to a successful conclusion. We are introduced to him as a man of intelligence, the reputed "cleverest" of the Greeks as well as the favorite of Athena, the goddess of wisdom. And in the *Odyssey*, again and again, he uses his ingenuity to save himself, as when he binds himself and his men to the bottom of the sheep of the Cyclops to escape his cave.

But he is not only a man of intelligence; he is also a man of courage who has fought long and hard in the Trojan War and whose courage and physical skill are always central to his adventures: Indeed, it is his physical prowess in the archery contest at the end of his wanderings that reveals his true identity to the suitors who are littering his ancestral home. And he is a man of beauty: His patroness Athena makes him taller and broader, and his curls "like thick hyacinth clusters full of blooms" so that the princess Nausicaa falls immediately in love with him. Later Athena does the same for his meeting with the faithful Penelope. Odysseus does not have to choose between intelligence and beauty, or between action and reflection, because he's not an American hero; he is allowed to have it all.

In his introduction to the 1996 Robert Fagles translation of the *Odyssey*, the classical scholar Bernard Knox makes the same point about Odysseus: He is a man known the world over for his *craft*, his cleverness, and his ability to deceive. But he is also a warrior whose code of honor and unflinching courage are equal to those of any Greek warrior. The appeal of the *Odyssey* is that the hero is an ideal version of everyman: He is not limited to one heroic quality, but he has every human quality, and thus speaks to the very human wish to be a complete person.

Classical scholars have always known that although the Greeks articulated the ideal forms of modern democracy, their vision of the ideal human was less than "democratic" in the American sense of a fair distribution of talents or special qualities. When I asked Mary Lefkowitz, the author of *Greek Gods*,

Human Lives, about whether the idea of nerds and geeks was reflected in Greek tradition, she answered as follows: "The Greeks did not require one to make a choice between beauty and brains. The best people had both, and the worst people were ugly and evil." She went on to point out the character of Thersites in the *Iliad*: The commoner Thersites is described as odd or funny-looking, and his speech in book 2 of the *Iliad* is, essentially, a model of cowardice. His reward for this speech is being beaten by Odysseus with the scepter of Agamemnon in front of the assembled Greek warriors. The Greek heroes were ideal men, allowed to be the best of everything, while people who were ugly or unattractive were punished. "The ugliest people," Lefkowitz says, "were picked to be the scapegoats, the ritual persons driven out to cleanse the community's pollution." It would have been unthinkable for a man of Odysseus's talents as a thinker to have been depicted as weird or nerdy or geeky.

Classic heroic literature, then, reminds us that when we are sick of literature featuring nerd/geek stereotypes, there is somewhere else to go. When we are choosing things for our kids to read, there *is* a literary tradition other than the "Man of Action versus Man of Reflection" dichotomy. But when kids choose for themselves, what do they choose? We can't always tell them what to read. Happily, we have another European hero for kids to emulate: another hero who does not have to choose between action and reflection. And it happens that that hero has single-handedly kept the publishing world afloat for several years.

Yes, it's Harry Potter. He's the junior wizard who gets to be the best at wizardry, the star, of sorts, at his school for wizards (even though his friend Hermione always does better at spells). And he is a star on the playing fields, being a natural "athlete" at the revered old game of Quidditch. For those who have not had the Potter experience, it is hard to capture the feeling of shock, when encountering him for the first time (either in the first book or in the first movie), to see what J. K. Rowling does with him. She makes him look, in American terms, "nerdy": He has those glasses, after all, and he is shy and awkward when he first goes to Hogwarts. For Americans, he pushes all the nerd buttons. So it is a complete, and very satisfying, revelation when he discovers that he is also an athletic superstar, supremely talented and courageous on the playing fields. Meeting Harry Potter for the first time is like traveling to another planet; he is a distinctly un-American hero. But somehow, he is not frozen out by American readers, especially kids. Kids love Harry Potter, and they seem to forgive him, and the woman who made him, by allowing him to enjoy all the several talents that violate the rigid rules of nerd/geek stereotypes.

There is another tradition, of course, in more contemporary American literature, television, and movies for kids: the "nerd-transcended" theme. Even the wretched *Beauty and the Geek* television show has the story line of nerds and geeks transcending their narrow confines: They gradually learn how to be cool, while at the same time the beauties are actually beginning to read books! Ever since the John Hughes teen movie *The Breakfast Club*, kids who are rigidly stereotypic have been inspirationally shedding their shackles by the final frame. They start out as walking, breathing stereotypes, and they eventually find real, nuanced life. Who could complain?

As we shall see later, there is good reason to complain. There is a vast difference between real, multidimensional heroes and cardboard people who become multidimensional. Part of that story has to do with how kids read cautionary tales concocted by adults: They often tend to pay attention to the "Here's how the world is" part and ignore the "But it can be different" part. If the "nerd transcended" theme is to have any benefit, kids have to pay attention to both the description of the stereotypical world and the miraculous transformation, and often they don't. They just get the first part, the instruction manual about the stereotypes themselves.

The other reason that stories about real, multidimensional heroes resonate with kids is that they are actually more like real life than the stereotypical versions of reality. Kids observe reality in an unvarnished form before their perceptual apparati are distorted by grown-up cultural lenses. Real kids, I believe, would recognize in an instant that Clark Kent is actually Superman; kids who haven't been indoctrinated don't know yet what they are supposed to see. There is a reason, after all, why Hans Christian Andersen chose a child to reveal that the emperor had no clothes. In a sense, nerd/geek stereotypes are as "real" as the emperor's clothes; there are no research data to suggest that intelligent or scholarly people are weak, sickly, unhealthy, or inherently unattractive. As we shall see, the physical characteristics implied by the nerd/geek stereotype were discredited by psychology research several decades ago.

But looking back at the historical dichotomies in American culture and looking at the contemporary dichotomies of nerds versus jocks, one would not know this. Indeed, if there is any directionality or movement in these dichotomies, it is in validating them. We are learning, with increasing regularity, that nerds and geeks are not just different; they are also sick. They have diagnoses that make them truly different from the rest of us, truly unwell. We can have compassion for them, of course, because they can't help it. But the tidal wave of pathologizing in contemporary American culture is sweeping up all the hapless nerds in its path. And if you think literature doesn't give nerds a chance, wait till you see what medicine has in store for them.

4.

THEY CAN'T HELP IT, THEY'RE JUST SICK

· OR ·

HOW BETTER TREATMENT MIGHT HELP CURE BILL GATES

Of course, high-functioning people on the spectrum have long attended college. Tony Attwood, a psychologist and author of *The Complete Guide to Asperger's Syndrome*, tells of trying to spot the professor with Asperger's when he's on the lecture circuit. That is, unless Dr. Attwood is at an engineering school, in which case he tries to spot the professors who don't have Asperger's.

I don't know Dr. Tony Attwood, but if I were an engineering professor, I might take umbrage at his observation, mentioned here in a *New York Times* article. Indeed, umbrage is what I would take, because I would be on the receiving end of a joke (and I believe that Dr. Attwood uses this as a laugh line) that is not really very funny. It is a joke that might make it difficult to recruit engineering students: "Come on down and pursue the career that is the chosen profession of crazy people!" is not exactly guaranteed to close the deal. But that's not the biggest reason the joke is unfunny. The joke is unfunny precisely because of what it tells us about models of mental health, about what we, contemporary Americans, consider the exemplar of the mentally healthy person. What this joke tells us, essentially, is that nerds and geeks are not just weird; they're also sick.

For those of you who have been hiding in your underground bunker for the past five years, Asperger's syndrome has zoomed to the top of the charts of mental health diagnoses du jour. Just as multiple-personality disorders were the media darlings of the 1980s and attention-deficit disorders the pop icons of the 1990s, so Asperger's syndrome (followed closely by childhood bipolar disorder) is the first diagnostic star of the twenty-first century. It seems everyone has it, or everyone knows someone who has it, or, more to the point here, everyone knows someone who is "a little Asperger's" or "a little Aspergy." Because, as our community of behavioral scientists tells us over and over again, Asperger's syndrome (AS), like most other diagnoses, comes in degrees. It's not a yes-or-no thing; it's a little-or-a-lot thing. It's like southerners have always known: There are not just white people and black people, there are also people with "a touch of the tarbrush." So there are now people who have a touch of AS, but they can, like people with a "touch of the tarbrush," try to "pass." And when they try to pass, they try to pass themselves off as . . . nerds. Or geeks. Or engineering professors. But they can't fool Dr. Tony Attwood, and they can't fool us.

The concept of mild forms of mental illness has become, by now, a staple of popular psychology. The older, more mysterious designation used in medicine to describe a subclinical version of an illness, *forme fruste*, has been replaced by "shadow syndrome," a term popularized by psychiatrist John Ratey in a 1997 book. Ratey's book goes on at great length about all the mild forms of mental illness that affect people in everyday life: people who can't control their tempers, people who are irritable, people who express odd or eccentric ideas, who are really suffering from mild forms of bipolar disorder or depression or schizophrenia. It is a compelling idea and one that goes a very long way toward removing any sense of personal responsibility from any mildly unhappy adult. Let's just say that in the ongoing debate in American psychiatry about whether or not there is such a thing as bad behavior that is different from mental illness, Ratey's book comes down very strongly on the "illness" side of the debate.

We learn, then, from popularizers like Ratey that nerds are sick: They are the people who have mild forms, or "shadow syndromes," of autism. Even Bill Gates, the übernerd to whom all nerds are compared, is diagnosed at a distance:

At present the classic autism shadow syndrome is undeniably male. And, social stereotyping aside, the most recognized embodiment of this shadow syndrome is the nerd. He is the computer programmer hunched over his monitor at all hours of the day and night, a pocket protector lodged permanently in his rumpled shirt. He has few or no friends; often he has no wife. He is a geek.

He is called "geek" or "nerd" or "wonk" for one reason alone: he is socially awkward. Out of it. Techie types have long recognized this quality in themselves: MIT actually offers a January course in social skills that students call "charm school." . . .

Nor has the connection between autism and computerdom gone unnoticed. *Time* magazine once ran an item comparing Microsoft's Bill Gates to the famous autistic savant Temple Grandin (Gates's reported autistic qualities included rocking, jumping on trampolines, not making eye contact, and not having the social skills necessary to enter a group conversation).

It is difficult to know where to begin when discussing caricature masquerading as science. But let's try, let's begin with the obvious. Ratey makes a vague claim that he will discuss nerds and geek with "social stereotyping aside." He then goes on to drag out the most tired signifier of the nerd stereotype, the pocket protector, as evidence of a nerd's complete lack of social skills. Hasn't it occurred to Ratey, or anyone else for that matter, that the pocket protector has a function as well as a meaning? Why would anyone wear a pocket protector in a "rumpled" shirt? Pocket protectors exist for the sole purpose of making sure that one does not ruin one's shirts by putting pens (which now have caps, so pocket protectors are a lot less necessary) or pencils (and most professionals who use a lot of pencils use retractable pencils, so, once again, the protector is unnecessary) in the pockets. Pocket protectors are used to protect clothing. So why would Ratey's nerd, in the "rumpled" shirt with the pocket protector lodged "permanently" in it, bother to use one? He's not interested in protecting his clothing. Why would he bother to protect a rumpled shirt?

The truth about pocket protectors is that they belong to a completely different definition, or attribute, of nerds and geeks. It is nonsensical to discuss pocket protectors as necessarily associated with a lack of social skill. Anyone who has been paying attention will notice that pocket protectors are always seen in beautifully laundered or ironed shirts: pocket protectors are practical and worldly things designed to make one's shirts last longer. They are in the same class as fanny packs and cords worn around the neck to hold one's reading glasses. They are functional objects, and they proclaim to the observer: I care more about practicality than I do about fashion. Pocket protectors, which are fading fast anyway, are a holdover from the days when dress shirts were expensive and pencil-wielding male professionals like teachers and engineers, who were (and still are) often underpaid, needed them to protect their investment in the shirts. *And they were often put there by these men's wives because they were the ones responsible for laundering the shirts and stretching the household budget.* We'll get back to those wives in a moment. For now let's notice that Ratey's nerds are just like everyone else's nerds, a blend of fact and fiction, of social observation and mythic archetype, which is fine if one is writing fiction but less so if one is supposedly, like Ratey, interested in close quasi-scientific observation.

Ratey's nerd is also marked for life by his lack of social skills: He has "few or no friends and often no wife." Anyone who has known nerds and geeks know that they often have a vast network of friends, some nearby and some online, who share their unusual interests. Frequently people labeled as nerds have to go a little further than others to find friends who share their interests, as eccentrics always have. The whole point of meetings of people with unusual interests, like conventions of *Star Trek* fans, is that unusual people—poets, psychoanalysts, Civil War reenactors, or burlesque artists, to name a few—can be just as enthusiastic, free, and unbounded in the expression of their shared passions as anyone else who goes to conventions or meetings. Like almost everyone else who uses the stereotype, Ratey confuses "few or no friends in eighth grade" with "few or no friends ever in life." And when it comes to the wives, Ratey may be even further off the mark. Of his own three cases discussed at length in *Shadow Syndromes*, men who all suffer from "mild forms of autism," two are married. One has been married three times and has three children, so, although he obviously has problems with relationships, he has enough social skill to woo and wed three different women, and he knows enough about sex to have had intercourse at least three times. Ratey's subjects all describe problems with dating, dealing with women who are interested in them, finding and keeping friends, understanding others and feeling understood. In other words, his "mildly autistic" patients bear almost no resemblance to the stereotypical nerd—the one with few or no friends and no wife—that he describes. It might be nitpicking here, but if his stock-in-trade is a humanistic commitment to understanding the inner lives of individuals, why does Ratey resort to such unspecific, broad-brush categorizations? Why does he state so baldly that nerds are more than a little sick?

IN SICKNESS AND IN HEALTH

We might locate Ratey's odd logic as part of the current zeitgeist of America's ostensibly compassionate mental-health establishment. In the bad old days of the 1950s, our current mental-health gurus tell us, all mental illnesses were blamed on bad upbringing: Both of the reigning psychological theories of the day, behaviorism and psychoanalysis, emphasized the role of pathogenic home environments in producing sick adults. Now we have come full circle, and biology is described, by biologically oriented psychiatrists and the public at large, as the leading cause of mental illness. In the seventies and eighties, "biological" causes were still reserved for serious mental illnesses: There were "endogenous" depressions, which were presumably more severe, biologically caused, and treated with antidepressants, and then there were "reactive" or "neurotic" depressions, which were seen as less severe, psychosocially caused, and treated with psychotherapy. But the ground shifted in 1993, with what we might call the beginning of the *forme fruste* movement, when Peter Kramer published his bestselling book *Listening to Prozac*. Kramer argued that all sorts of chronic and characterological problems like irritability, fits of temper, or lethargy were mild forms of depression that might profitably be treated biomedically, that is, with psychoactive medications. For Kramer, this was real compassion: Finally, people could come to understand that their difficulties, even mild difficulties, were the result of their biology and *no one's fault.*

The societal transformation brought about by the *forme fruste* movement has been astonishing. The cute or terrifying advertisements for every possible human complaint, from social anxiety to depression-related physical pain, are omnipresent on television and in magazines. Profits for pharmaceutical companies have gone through the roof in the last two decades. But more important, the commonsense definition of the relationship between mental illness and mental health has changed dramatically, a development that is passionately advocated by *forme frustes* like Peter Kramer and John Ratey.

Historically, this compassionate shift was instigated by none other than Sigmund Freud. It was Freud who wrote the book with one of the best titles ever devised, *The Psychopathology of Everyday Life*, in which he began his lifelong project of demonstrating that the mechanisms that produced most mental illnesses were identical to the processes of normal everyday thinking and coping. This was a compassionate statement in a time when the mentally ill were most emphatically seen as "other." The universal psychological mechanisms described by Freud have been replaced by the universal biological mechanisms of the *forme fruste* movement, but the message is the same: We're all a little mentally ill. One could argue about the inflections here. For Freud, the conclusion to be drawn from the universality of these mechanisms was that we should treat the mentally ill with compassion, because they are just like us. For the *forme frustes*, the conclusion to be drawn is that we should all get treatment, because we are just like them. But the underlying humanism of the argument is the same.

Yet there's a problem. As with most nuanced arguments, the nuance is metabolized in a less-than-nuanced form in the popular press and eventually in popular opinion. As we have seen, social stereotypes like nerds and geeks are not initially nuanced, because they are learned by kids who do not think in a nuanced fashion: Kids learn that there are nerds and geeks, and then there's "us," and that these two categories are radically different. They don't get the whole spectrum thing, because that's not how kids think. So in the pre–*forme fruste* movement days, kids might have been called nerds or geeks and seen as devalued people, kids who were weird and different and inadequate: They were the other, but they were not necessarily sick. Now, kids get the trickle-down message that nerds and geeks have something like mild autism or Asperger's syndrome or some other syndrome. The nuanced version of this is that millions of people may suffer from mild versions of mental illness, that there is a continuum, not a bright line, between "normal" and "sick." Crabby people might have mild forms of depression; shy or nerdy people might have some mild form of autism. But sending a nuanced message to a person who is more literal minded is not often so successful. Kids, and less nuanced grown-ups, just get the message that, in addition to nerds being weird, they are also sick. And then they are subject to all the prejudices that sick people are subject to. The message is lost in translation: Instead of the compassionate dictum that the sick are not the other, kids get the message that the nerds, the other, are even more "other," because they are sick.

This happens with wearing regularity every time an autistic or autistic-like kid commits a crime. It is impossible for the contemporary media to report these events without using the stereotype; there is something irresistible in the journalistic trope "you know the kind of kid we're talking about . . . you know, the nerdy kind of kid." When a suburban Boston teenager with Asperger's syndrome allegedly killed a classmate in January 2007, somehow the *Boston Herald* managed to get through the headline without using The Trope. The cover of the tabloid read: "STUNNED. Cops: Baby-Faced Teen Slaughtered Classmate in School Bathroom." Even in the main story, we learned simply that the alleged killer suffers from Asperger's syndrome. But in the section "Experts: Teen Years Tough for Asperger's Sufferers," we read the social side of the story:

> Specialists say teenagers with Asperger's Syndrome—a high-functioning form of autism—are almost always "mercilessly teased" in school and rebuffed by classmates because of poor social skills.
>
> "Children with Asperger's have poor friendship and relationship skills and are often rejected by a lot of kids and made to feel awful whenever they are at school," said Lynda Geller, clinical director of the Asperger Institute at the NYU Child Study Center in New York.
>
> The defense attorney for sixteen-year-old John Odgren—the Lincoln-Sunbury High School student charged yesterday with stabbing to death a classmate—said the teen suffers from Asperger's Syndrome.
>
> "Students with the brain disorder often are teased because of their public awkwardness. They're seen as geeky and odd, don't know how to joke or when to stop, or how to interact with the opposite sex," Geller said.

Okay. All true. And so compassionate, sort of. Thank you, Dr. or Ms. Geller, for your words of wisdom, but is there a reason you have to mention geeks? I know you said, *"They're seen as* geeky and odd," which is all true, but don't you spend enough time with regular kids to know what this means to regular kids? If alleged killer kids with Asperger's syndrome are seen as geeky and odd, then by the commutative property of kid stereotyping, what are geeky or odd kids seen as? You got it . . . potential killers. Isn't there a way we can talk about real kids with real, and rare, problems like Asperger's without implying that all geeky kids, or even all AS sufferers, are ticking time bombs just waiting to stab an innocent classmate? I don't know about you, but if Dr. Tony Attwood is correct and all professors in engineering schools suffer from Asperger's syndrome, I'm staying away; Cal Tech or MIT are probably just bloodbaths waiting to happen.

ASPERGER'S SYNDROME: THE REAL THING

It might be helpful here to focus on Asperger's syndrome as a real thing: the genuine article, not the *forme fruste*. Asperger's syndrome is named after the Austrian psychiatrist and neurologist Hans Asperger, who published a paper in 1944 describing a constellation of symptoms he saw in a number of child patients who had some, but not all, of the diagnostic features usually associated with autism. These child patients had impairments in social skills and some of the signature behaviors of autistic patients, like spinning in circles, arm-flapping, and other self-stimulating behaviors. But, unlike classic autistic children, Asperger's patients had normal intelligence and language development. The diagnosis was lurking around for years, but it was not until 1994 that it made the big time, in the fourth edition of the *Diagnostic and Statistical Manual of Mental Disorders*, the bible of the mental-health business, known in the trade as the *DSM-IV* (*DSM-IV-TR*, for the latest update).

The *DSM-IV* is not just a diagnostic manual; it is *the*

diagnostic manual for the entire field of American mental health. It serves as the final word for doctors, insurance companies, and researchers by providing agreed-on and field-tested criteria for all mental-health diagnoses, so that, when people are talking about a specific diagnosis, they can be relatively certain they are talking about the same thing. So the diagnostic criteria in the manual are very specific and make it possible to say with some degree of certainty (or at least "reliability," as defined by agreement among professionals in the field) whether one "has" or "does not have" a mental illness. This is not to say that the *DSM-IV* endorses a black or white view of these disorders. It is certainly possible, in our *DSM* world, to have *some* of the symptoms of, say, schizophrenia or bipolar disorder, but if not enough of these symptoms are present, not enough of the diagnostic criteria are met to warrant either of the labels. The *DSM-IV* does not deny the existence of *formes frustes*, but its stated purpose is to draw the bright lines between full clinical presentations and subclinical presentations of psychiatric diagnoses.

The diagnostic criteria for Asperger's syndrome, that is, the official criteria as listed in the Book, are as follows:

A. Qualitative impairment in social interaction, as manifested by at least two of the following:
  (1) marked impairments in the use of multiple nonverbal behaviors such as eye-to-eye gaze, facial expression, body postures, and gestures to regulate social interaction
  (2) failure to develop peer relationships appropriate to developmental level

   (3) a lack of spontaneous seeking to share enjoyment, interests, or achievements with other people (e.g., by a lack of showing, bringing, or pointing out objects of interest to other people)

   (4) lack of social or emotional reciprocity

B. Restricted repetitive and stereotyped patterns of behavior, interests, and activities, as manifested by at least one of the following:

   (1) encompassing preoccupation with one or more stereotyped and restricted patterns of interest that is abnormal either in intensity or focus

   (2) apparently inflexible adherence to specific, nonfunctional routines or rituals

   (3) stereotyped and repetitive motor mannerisms (e.g., hand or finger flapping or twisting, or complex whole-body movements)

   (4) persistent preoccupation with parts of objects

C. The disturbance causes clinically significant impairment in social, occupational, or other important areas of functioning.

D. There is no clinically significant general delay in language (e.g., single words used by age 2 years, communicative phrases used by age 3 years).

E. There is no clinically significant delay in cognitive development or in the development of age-appropriate self-help skills, adaptive behavior (other than social interaction), and curiosity about the environment in childhood.

F. Criteria are not met for another specific Pervasive Developmental Disorder or Schizophrenia.

These criteria are extremely useful in documenting who really does suffer from Asperger's syndrome and who does not. There certainly are kids who suffer greatly from this illness, and their families probably suffer even more. In my own work as a child therapist I encounter a child every now and then who meets enough diagnostic criteria to warrant the label of AS, but it's pretty rare. The base rates in the population, as accurately as we can tell now, are actually very low. This is another good thing about the *DSM-IV*: It contains statistics on prevalence estimates or the approximate rates of appearance of a specific mental illness in the general population. At the time of the publication of the *DSM-IV* in 1994, there was little or no reliable research on the prevalence of AS. The prevalence of full-blown autism, which shares some behavioral features with AS, was thought to be, in 1994, two to five cases per 10,000 individuals, or .05 percent at most.

Since then, however, the prevalence of AS and autism in the general population appears to be skyrocketing. A review study published in *Public Health Reports* in 2004 demonstrated that the rate of autism climbed from approximately 3 cases per 10,000 in the 1970s to a rate of 30 cases per 10,000 during the 1990s. The rate of autistic-spectrum disorders (including AS) appears to have increased from approximately 5 per 10,000 in the 1970s to a rate of 50 per 10,000 in the late 1990s. These studies controlled for "case-finding" issues: The possibility that there are just more cases being found or that diagnostic criteria are not being strictly applied does not seem to be a factor in the huge increase in rates of autism. Autism researchers continue to suggest, in stronger and stronger terms, that there is some environmental factor contributing to these increases, something about which we should all be in a mild state of panic.

But what about that prevalence of AS? The question here is fuzzier, at least as far as rigorous epidemiologists see it. Definitional problems—AS is sometimes called "high-functioning autism"—make it difficult to know who has what or how many people really have it at all. As with any diagnosis, the closer one gets to the normal end of the spectrum, or the normal range of functioning, the harder it is to identify "true" cases. If Asperger's syndrome really is high-functioning autism, then it is the high-functioning part that gets in the way of diagnostic clarity; if they are high-functioning, why does it make sense to talk about people as suffering from an illness at all?

We can learn a lesson here from the last superstar diagnosis, attention-deficit disorder, which has similar problems in establishing prevalence rates. When rates of ADD and rates of children medicated for ADD were skyrocketing in the 1980s and 1990s, questions were raised again and again about whether stringent diagnostic criteria were being systematically applied. Kids who were "a little ADD" were getting medicated along with kids whose parents just wanted their kids to have a little performance-enhancing medication. As medication rates rose, ADD mavens were hard-pressed to explain why there seemed to be a sudden rise in what was supposed to be a neurological disorder. Either more "true" kids were being diagnosed (in which case we needed to have some biological explanation for the epidemic) or more "false" kids were being medicated, and it was impossible to tell which was which.

In the subsequent effort to explain huge increases in the diagnosis of and medication for ADD, questionable and even pseudoscientific explanations abounded in the national mental-health community. In my own home region of still semirural western New England, I publicly questioned the ballooning rates of ADD diagnoses and medications, which appeared to be far above national prevalence rates. But a local physician explained to me, with a perfectly straight face, that in western New England we had more than our share of congenitally "restless" people, those who had left Boston two hundred years ago and settled in the western mountains, and that, therefore, their progeny, still congenitally "restless," had higher rates of ADD.[*] But as an explanation, the restless-settlers explanation is somewhat more palatable than the alternatives, like the relentless-marketing-by-pharmaceutical-companies explanation.

The problem with making reliable ADD diagnoses is that they are very frequently made in comparison to a small group. Teachers who know a little but not enough about psychiatric disorders may observe that there is a kid in their own classroom who is particularly jumpy, the jumpiest kid in the class. He may be suspected of having ADD and put on medication and to stop him from being jumpy. But then there will be someone else who is now noticeably jumpy. If this kid is now suspected of "having" ADD—after all, he is now the jumpiest kid in the class—maybe he "has" ADD, too. Pretty soon you're getting false prevalence rates of 20, 25, or 30 percent of kids in

_____

[*]It was never explained to me why these restless settlers didn't move on to Montana, or why people in Colorado or California don't just get it over with and put Ritalin in the drinking water.

a school being treated for ADD, far above the official prevalence rate of 5 to 7 percent in elementary-school populations.
If restlessness alone is taken as the major diagnostic criterion,
it is almost inevitable that there will be far too many false positive diagnoses.

That's why the *DSM-IV* includes, for every psychiatric
diagnosis, functional impairment as a criterion. If a kid is
jumpy, that may be a problem for a teacher, but if his jumpiness is not associated with significant functional impairment,
like problems with friends or problems with grades, then he
doesn't have the illness. His jumpiness is then, officially, a
quirk, *because it's not getting in his way*. It is defined as normal
variation, like height: Kids can be various heights, but there
are few conditions involving height that contribute to functional impairment.

Asperger's syndrome works the same way. In order to "have"
Asperger's syndrome, you *must* have two of the symptoms
listed under part (A) of the criteria listed earlier, and you *must*
have one of the symptoms listed under part (B); furthermore,
you *must* meet all the conditions outlined in parts (C) through
(F). If you don't meet all those conditions, you don't have it.
There are several conditions relevant to our discussion here,
but the most important for our purposes is (C). Condition (C)
specifies "clinically significant impairment in social, occupational, or other important areas of functioning." When Dr. Tony
Attwood surveys all those engineering professors, he is presumably not surveying a population of people who have "clinically
significant impairment in occupational functioning," because
they're not unemployed or underemployed; *they're engineering
professors*. Therefore he must be able to tell, just from looking

at them, that they all have clinically significant impairments in social or "other" important areas of functioning. Now that's what I call diagnostic acuity.

This might seem like nerdy or Aspergy nitpicking, but it's important: It's functional impairment itself that makes a sick person sick as opposed to well. One of the major reasons for the revision of the *DSM* was the failure in its earlier version (*DSM-III*) to emphasize that "functional impairment" criterion of illness. As a result of that underemphasis, lots of people were "diagnosed" with mental disorders who were just regular folks, walking around doing their jobs, marrying, raising families, paying taxes, and dying like everyone else but doing these activities in an unusual way. The emphasis on "functional impairment" in the new version reduces the number of people who "are" mentally ill by officially recognizing that being unusual is not an illness.

This brings us back to the übernerd. How is it that people like John Ratey can describe Bill Gates as having autistic qualities? The implication is that he suffers from some version of an extremely debilitating illness. Is it because Gates occasionally jumps, or once jumped, on trampolines? If that is so, then all those girls on the late and not-too-lamented *Man Show*, the scantily clad girls who jumped on trampolines as the credits rolled, must also be hiding something: their secret autistic tendencies. How can it be possible that the world's richest individual—someone who suffers less from "occupational impairment" than any other person on the planet—could be described as suffering from some form of high-functioning autism?

Ratey is not the only one who makes this diagnosis (and, after all, he was just quoting *Time* magazine). The actor John Schneider has started his own foundation to promote awareness of Asperger's syndrome. Here's what *USA Today* reported about his work in April 2003:

> On *Smallville*, John Schneider plays the father of teenager Clark Kent. In real life, Schneider is dad to his 11-year-old son, Chasen, who also has incredible abilities. "My son has Asperger's syndrome, which is part of the autism spectrum," says Schneider, who is best known for starring on the *Dukes of Hazzard*. "It's likely Albert Einstein had Asperger's, and so did Thomas Jefferson. Bill Gates I'm certain has it. With many highly motivated successful people that have done something in an obscure area, you're going to find an 'odd bird' now and then."

No, John, Bill Gates does not meet the diagnostic criteria for Asperger's syndrome. Condition (C) specifically refers to clinically significant impairment in social, occupational, or other areas of functioning. It's not occupational impairment, so it must be "clinically significant social impairment" that gets him the diagnosis from Dr. Dukes of Hazzard, right? One never knows the true heart of a man from a biography, but the official Microsoft Corporation biography of Bill Gates notes that he started the company with his childhood friend, Paul Allen, and that he met Steve Ballmer in his dorm hallway while he was a Harvard student. The guy has had some friends, and he is married and has three children. Where's the impairment? If he has lifelong friends and a wife and children, what is he lacking that could be described as impairment?

THE MAN OF CONVERSATION

Oh, that's right. There's that social thing. Bill Gates's gaze is reported to be not quite normal, and the cadence of his speech is sometimes reported to be flat. These must comprise the "clinically significant impairment" that gets him the diagnosis of Asperger's syndrome. One might notice here that the American Man of Action we have celebrated throughout our history may be in the process of modification himself: The new ideal American man may be the Man of Conversation. Because what gets all these guys (and they are still mostly guys) the label—whether it be the label of "nerd" or "geek" or of Asperger's syndrome—are apparent anomalies of social skills. The implication in all this armchair diagnosis is that it is not enough to be able to make millions or billions of dollars, and it is not enough to find a mate who shares your passions and who will carry your genes into future generations. It is also imperative that children as well as adults be able to look people in the eye for a specified "normal" amount of time when they speak. The American man must essentially have a firm handshake and a smile, or he is not a normal American man. And even if the American man has billions of dollars and friends and a wife and children, if he doesn't look people in the eye, he's still got that pesky syndrome.

Eventually, of course, all discussions of psychiatric diagnosis must involve discussions of what is culturally allowable.

Who decides what is sick and what is not has always been a question of power and the enforcement of the values of the powerful. Outsiders and gadflies in the American mental-health community have always known this, and have made note of the fact that women and minorities have always been labeled as "sick" by a medical establishment that enshrines the values of one segment of society while making assertions of scientific objectivity. In a brilliant and iconoclastic 1994 article in *Skeptic* titled "The Illusion of Science in Psychiatry," Carol Tavris described a real nineteenth-century mental "illness," drapetomania, or the irrational desire of slaves to run away from their owners. Tavris goes on to deconstruct many of the ways in which diagnoses are made, making the case that it usually amounts to who is complaining about whom. Slaves, for example, were probably not complaining to doctors about some bizarre condition that was showing up in white people that gave them the irrational conviction that they could hold title to human beings. But runaway slaves were a problem for the powerful, and the compassionate among them decided that this condition must be an illness. And illness, then as now, carries with it the notion of a lack of culpability along with the potential for cure.

A more contemporary example of the social construction of mental illness is, of course, homosexual behavior. Homosexuality was dropped from the *Diagnostic and Statistical Manual of Mental Disorders* in its third edition, which appeared in 1973. Before that, being gay was officially a sickness; after that, it was not. While this was a salutary development for advocates for gay rights, it did underline the socially constructed or just plain arbitrary nature of the way our society officially decides what illness is. Since this is a medical model, after all, we might have hoped that the biological underpinnings of such a model might have precluded fashion or political correctness from the decision about what got in and what got left out.

So, if mental illnesses can be recategorized when social conditions change, how about recategorizing social-skills deficits as markers of illness? As I have argued, it is already intellectually untenable to be handing out diagnoses of Asperger's syndrome like Halloween candy, especially to people who are both professionally and personally successful. If personal peculiarity is the only remaining marker of illness, why should it be called an illness at all? Maybe personal peculiarity, or a lack of "adequate" eye contact or vocal inflection, is a stigmatized behavior, like homosexual behavior, that needs simply to be officially destigmatized. In an age when success depends less and less on social contact, the necessity for these skills is already decreasing. Why not make it official?

THE NERD GENOCIDE

Okay, maybe the term "genocide" is too strong, but if nerdity is a condition that, like homosexuality, is thought to be biologically based and still (unlike homosexuality) officially an "illness" of some kind, then we have to decide whether or not we want to cure it. If Asperger's syndrome is a mild form of autism, in the near future we might be facing the possibility of genetic manipulations that would eliminate the possibility of having an autistic child and therefore the possibility of having a child with Asperger's syndrome, or maybe even any quirky person who might be labeled a nerd. Is that what we want?

These questions are discussed in a seminal article by Steve Silberman, "The Geek Syndrome," which appeared in *Wired* magazine in 2001. Silberman takes on all the current hot-button issues: the rising prevalence of autism and Asperger's syndrome, especially in California and especially in Silicon Valley. If it's not mercury poisoning, might something else be contributing to the rise in the reported cases of all these syndromes? Silberman suggests it might, indeed, be a problem of "assortative mating." In the historical past, this argument goes, nerdy/geeky/Aspergy people were few, and their social-skills deficits may have prevented them from finding mates and passing on their "geek genes." But now, there are more female geeks, and the concentration of such people in a few job categories and geographic areas (like Silicon Valley and the Route 495 corridor outside Boston) makes it easier for them to find each other. They then mate with each other, in a process population biologists call "assortative mating"—the tendency for people with certain genetic characteristics to marry each other. Silberman suggests that the explosion of cases of autism and AS in Silicon Valley might be the result of all these formerly nonprocreating people suddenly procreating, and by so doing their mild forms of autism are magnified in the next generation, because their children have a double dose of geek genes.

This argument rests on several questionable assumptions, including those issues about case-finding and false-positive diagnoses in cases of syndromes like AS, which are, by definition, marked by high functioning. If indeed all these former social isolates are now making millions of dollars and reproducing like rabbits, describing them as suffering from an illness at all becomes more problematic, as we have seen. But, as Silberman points out, if the problem really is genetic, are people really going to look to a bright future when we have selective breeding to produce more people with great eye contact and melodious voices and fewer people like Thomas Jefferson or Bill Gates? Would we expect nerds and geeks to participate in their own genocide? Homosexuals who worry about these kinds of things are already up in arms about research in the animal world that *may*, at some point in the future, lead to a genetic or hormonal cure for the problem of gay sheep. The question "If gay sheep can be cured, are gay people far behind?" leads directly to the term "gay genocide."

But, if there were a nerd genocide, it would need to be endorsed not only by parents of nerds-in-utero but also by nerds themselves. In this case, the genocide would have to be invented and carried out by the very people it might seek to extinguish. While geneticists are already working on the problem of the genetic bases of autism, it seems less likely that these same people (intellectuals and scientists who may presumably have some heightened empathy for nerds if they are not "actually" nerds themselves) will enthusiastically embrace the disappearance of their kind from the face of the earth. A more prudent and more humane response to the problem of the "geek syndrome" would be to abolish it legislatively by dropping some, if not all, social-skills deficits from the official manual of mental illness. This will not happen, of course, until there are enough nerdy people who rise up, as homosexuals did in the past, and demand an end to official stigmatization. It may not happen in our lifetimes, but it will happen if only for the simple reason that many social-skills deficits will be less and less debilitating in the future.

When asked for the definition of a mentally healthy person, Sigmund Freud once gave the simple answer that a mentally healthy person was one who had the ability to "love and work." We may be entering a new era, when nerds and geeks, and even people with illnesses like Asperger's syndrome, can love and work, and make babies as well as computer code. We may also be entering an era when people who have excellent social skills but little ability or inclination for focused work in the symbolic realm cannot love and work. They may be able to love, but the work part may get harder and harder for the man whose primary skill is conversation. We still need talk-show hosts and presidents, so that day is still a long way off. But the direction of material success as well as power is all on the side of nerds and geeks, and sooner or later they will rewrite the DSM as well. And when they do, they may just decide to write nerdity out of the book. Antinerd prejudices will not go away overnight, but then, at least officially, they will go away.

5.

THE SEINFELD AXIOM

· OR ·

WHY NERDS KNOW ADVANCED CALCULUS BUT CAN'T GET TO FIRST BASE

Was your last 'intimate relationship' in a chat room?" If you said yes, add a point to your nerd self-test score. Or your geek self-test score: As we know, you know you're a geek when . . . "Deodorant is as foreign a concept as toothpaste or mouthwash," or "Your mom is the only woman to ever see the inside of your bedroom," or "You know more URLs than girls' phone numbers." One of the few things we know for sure is that nerds and geeks have a lot of trouble getting laid. If we read the self-tests, we can figure out why this might be so: They are awkward, don't use deodorant, don't pay enough attention to their appearance, can't dance, and spend too much time with their moms. We know this . . . Wait a minute, why *do* we know this? We know this because we know about nerds, and we know they are unappealing *by definition*. But what do we observe about people who are interested in science and technology or like to do well in school or like *Star*

Trek before we "know" that they are nerds? Is there something real that corresponds to their near-mythic unattractiveness? More to the point, when kids are learning the nerd stereotype, why do they come to believe that nerds are so unappealing, especially since, as we shall see, it's so seldom true?

THE SEINFELD AXIOM

Let's take a trip back in time. It is season eight of *Seinfeld*, in the fall of 1996. In an episode titled "The Abstinence," George Costanza's girlfriend is suffering from mononucleosis, so they can't have sex for six weeks. During that time, George becomes more and more intelligent. The abstinence somehow contributes to his increasing brilliance, and of course the converse is implied: Sex makes him stupid or, more to the point, sex is what has been making him stupid. George gives batting advice to the New York Yankees, starts learning Portuguese, aces *Jeopardy!* and masters a Rubik's cube. Jerry invites him to give a talk for Career Day at their old junior high school. While he abstains from sex, George is positively delighted with himself in showing off his newfound intelligence, as if thinking is truly a satisfaction on a par with sex. The word "nerd" is not used in the episode, but the characterization is pretty familiar: George, when he stops having sex, starts acting like a nerd or a geek, especially in his enthusiastic willingness to expound (brilliantly) at the drop of a hat even if no one else is interested. At the end of the episode, however, George shows up at Career Day being his old stupid self, and Jerry realizes too late that George's abstinence is over.

This is what I call "the Seinfeld Axiom." It can be stated with utter simplicity: It says, "sex makes you stupid." The converse of the Seinfeld Axiom is: "Abstinence from sex makes you smart." The reason this plays out in such hilarious fashion in Jerry's world is that it is a piece of folk wisdom that is as old as time. It is something everybody knows, in his or her own way, and so its appearance in comic form on Seinfeld is like the appearance of an old friend or enemy, as the case may be. Because the Seinfeld Axiom is a just-barely-conscious piece of wisdom, it also can make the nerd stereotype seem, somehow, true. Somehow it makes sense that nerds aren't going to have a lot of sex, because if they did, they would be stupid like the rest of us, or, since they're not stupid like the rest of us, they must not be getting it very often.

At least as long ago as the ancient Greeks, the struggle between reason and passion, between the rule of law and the misrule of love, between the Apollonian and the Dionysian approach to living, has been a theme of great tragedies, comedies, and philosophical systems. In the *Phaedrus,* for example, Plato describes the structure of the human soul as being like a chariot with two horses: One horse is temperate, reasonable, and pure, while the other is wild and unmanageable. The task of the charioteer is to balance the powers of both horses and to steer a course powered by the energy of both. The metaphor serves to illuminate Plato's distinction between the two mortal parts of the human soul: the part embodied in the heart (the rational, pure part of the soul) and the part embodied in the belly (the animal longings of the soul). The parts of the soul are unchangeable givens, but, as with much ancient philosophy, the ideal state is one of balance between the two powerful opposing forces. A triumph of one power leads to the corresponding diminution of the other, and it is also true that a triumph of one power is *occasioned by* the diminution of the other. So George's turning into a genius when he stops having sex makes perfect sense in a Platonic kind of way: One horse is hobbled, and thus the power of the other is temporarily in the ascendant.

This Platonic idea has found its way into every form of psychology, which is, after all, the modern equivalent of Plato's systematic study of the soul (or *psyche* in the original Greek). Almost every kind of systematic theory in the history of psychology divides the human function of passion and the function of reason in some explicitly metaphorical or ostensibly literal fashion. In older psychology, the Platonic metaphor is more explicitly metaphorical, but in every explication of the metaphor of balanced or opposing forces, there are cases of people in only one of the contrasted states of mind: either people carried away by passion or people carried away by reason. These can be alternating states of mind in the same person, but each version of Platonically inspired psychology gives an account of persons who are chronically in a state of passion or a state of reason. And those who are chronically in a state of reason—those who spend too much time thinking— are certainly not getting carried away in transports of ecstasy.

In fact, they seem to be ecstatically reasonable: George, when he abstains from sex, is thrilled with himself as he uses his newfound intelligence, as if thinking were intoxicating.

GEORGE COSTANZA'S PSYCHOLOGY

In Freudian psychology at the turn of the twentieth century, the explicit dichotomy was between instinct and defense against instinct. Since the instincts were always sexual (at least before 1920, when Freud became convinced of the reality of the death instinct), the defenses were always defenses against becoming aware of sexual instincts. This was true even in earliest infancy: Indeed, for Freud, the whole structure of human thought was built on the opposition of the gratification of sexual instincts on one hand and the mechanisms of control and defense on the other. Literally the first thought, for Freud, was a compensatory hallucination: When the hungry infant could not have the (sexual) satisfaction of having the mother's breast, he or she would hallucinate the breast instead. In a very real sense, for Freud, representation itself came into being as a way of surviving the gaps between moments of instinctual gratification.

Later, Freud added to this theoretical notion when he articulated the notion of sublimation. Sublimation was described as a defense against becoming aware of disavowed sexual wishes as well as a defense against the feelings of deprivation and loss attendant on the nonfulfillment of those wishes. All the complex cultural achievements of humankind, whether literature or art, science or philosophy, were complex constructions people made as a result of not getting what they "really" wanted. Freud thought that all this sublimation was necessary; civilization itself was both a product of sublimation and the locus of the repression that made sublimation inevitable. It is worthy of note that cultural critics who blame "Freudianism" for the eroticization of contemporary culture are simply wrong when making these accusations. Although some of Freud's followers[*] claimed that civilization would be improved by a thorough, society-wide attack on sexual repression, Freud himself thought repression was a necessary evil as well as contributory to the greatest cultural achievements of humankind.

Some may look askance at the reductionism involved in Freud's initial theorizing. After all, he seems to be saying that people will choose sex if they can get it, and if they can't, then and only then will they paint the Sistine Chapel or write *Così fan tutte*. But his theorizing was greatly influenced by his reading of Darwin and what he saw as evolutionary biology's insistence on the expression of procreative instincts as the chief function of humans. In this, he is really very similar to the evolutionary biologists of today, who retain the same allegiance to the primacy of the biological imperative. If the chief end of man is "getting as many of one's genes as possible into succeeding generations," then many cultural phenomena would seem to be irrelevant at best. The field now known as evolutionary psychology has taken up the challenge of explaining

---

[*]Most notably Wilhelm Reich.

how everything that people do, no matter how unsexy, is really designed to further that end. But some of the theories set forth by evolutionary psychology to explain complex cultural phenomena are as tortured and as reductionist as anything Freud ever offered. Take the example of music, a human phenomenon notoriously difficult for evolutionary psychologists to explain. Why should people "waste" all that time and energy making music when they should be making babies? How does music-making further the primary evolutionary goal? No one knows, but that doesn't stop evolutionary psychologists from creating yet another of what the field's detractors call its multitudinous "Just So Stories." In the case of the evolutionary significance of music, these speculations usually end up with a wearily familiar reference to the sexual exploits of rock stars to clinch the explanation that all musical activity is simply a form of sexual display designed to get potential partners into the sack.

This theoretical opposition of sex and thinking is not only a Freudian thing or an evolutionary biology thing; this dichotomy is also reflected in much of classic developmental psychology. In observing kids and how they develop, many adults are struck by the opposition in developing teens of sexual wishes and behavior on one hand and reason and prudence on the other. The commonsense vulgarity of "thinking with your dick" expresses what many parents and developmental psychologists struggle to explain. In developmental psychology, this is usually expressed in some form of opposition of adequate psychological development in adolescence and pseudoadult sexual activity. Many developmental psychologists argue that a premature introduction to sexual intercourse necessarily means that intellectual development becomes stunted or less mature—another elegant version of the Sein- feld Axiom.

This is the position taken by followers of Piaget, for example, when they discuss the notion of premature structuralization. Piaget's theory of intellectual development is not a maturational theory: mature problem-solving abilities, for Piaget, result from open-ended interactions with the surrounding environment. Just getting older, for Piaget, doesn't make you smarter. There- fore, an ideal Piagetian course of development is one in which children's curiosity about problems in the physical and social world is preserved and nurtured as long as possible so that more sophisticated reasoning can supersede more childish reasoning. "Premature structuralization" is the name Piagetians have given to the phenomenon of kids' becoming adult too soon. It includes having sexual intercourse as well as working in jobs typically held by adults and trying to support their own children. A simple way of saying this, of course, is that kids who try to convince themselves they are adult by having sex, having babies, and sup- porting families are more likely to drop out of school and stop thinking in an open-ended way. A more complicated way of say- ing this is that all primate species have long periods of immatu- rity so that the young can retain the capacity for open-ended problem-solving, and when they become "adult," there is an aspect of development that is necessarily foreclosed, so that the energy that was going into figuring out new ways to grapple with the known world now goes into routinized ways of feeding and caring for the young. The revised version of the Seinfeld Axiom, for these theorists, is that it's not specifically sex that makes you stupid; it's parenting that makes you stupid. But often these things do go hand in hand.

The point is, the age-old Platonic opposition of reason and passion can find its way into almost any theoretical statement in psychology. It is as if "everyone knows" that sex and thinking are polar opposites, and theorizers are simply trying to figure out the way to make what "everyone knows" into a psychological theory. But developmental psychologists as well as parents have an urgent emotional investment in these polar oppositions. It is as if the urgent need to prevent teenagers from engaging in sexual experimentation is a deeply felt imperative in search of a theory to justify it. There are many reasons why kids should not start having sex too early, but parents are never very good at explicating them. The visceral sense of "They're too young for that" can be translated into all kinds of reasons, some given to kids directly and some whispered by parents to each other or verbalized to the self. Some of these reasons are religious: It is against God's law to enjoy sex outside the marriage contract. For more secular parents, the physical health of the child is invoked: Sex will give you a bad disease. Or it becomes an issue of intellectual health: If you have sex, someone will get pregnant, and schooling will be threatened. Emotional health is often invoked: There is the vague sense (always too vague for teenagers) that adding sex to a relationship will make it more hurtful when it ends. Added to this list is the less conscious but still powerful wisdom embodied in the Seinfeld Axiom: You shouldn't be having sex, because sex makes you stupid. You start thinking about sex, and you stop thinking about everything else. Parents believe that teenagers think about sex all the time anyway, but if they start really having sex, then they really won't think about anything else. And a century of psychological theory provides justification for what parents feel in their gut. But is there any evidence that sex and thinking really are so mutually exclusive? And if not, why are nerd/geek stereotypes so insistent on this point?

LICENSE TO LOVE

To try to understand this question in another way, we need to step into the murky waters of social science research. Nerds and geeks don't get any love action, the self-tests say, because they are basically unattractive. But what exactly does that mean? Social science can really be very unclear, especially when it comes to a concept like "attractiveness." Social psychologists have been muddying these waters since the 1970s, trying to understand the concept of "attractiveness" and why it works, because it does work. Carefully controlled research has shown that people rated as "attractive" by others—even if the others are total strangers—have more sex and more varied sex than those rated as less attractive (the evidence is more equivocal when looking at the actual number of sexual partners). But "attractive" people also have better jobs, make more money, and have more life satisfaction than others. So it's obviously not all about sex; it's about something more than sex.

Research that investigates the concept of "attractiveness" is tricky because of the methodology involved. It's like any survey research: The answers differ, and may differ greatly, depending on the precise way the questions are asked. Rating photographs of people, judging how "attractive" they are on a simple scale of one to seven, is simple indeed, but of course that is not how judgments of attractiveness are made. Real people make these judgments based on a complex series of cues—visual, of course, but also contextual—and thus the measurement issues become much more complex. And then there are what social scientists call the "halo effects": People who have been judged to be "attractive" are subsequently judged to be better-looking, kinder, and even more intelligent than those judged to be less attractive. In so doing, real people, at least in these carefully controlled laboratory conditions, seem to be giving the lie to the Seinfeld axiom: If sex doesn't actually make you smarter, sexiness makes you seem smarter, not dumber.

But it is the social-skills factor that really makes the judgments of attractiveness fly off the charts. It is not raw good looks that make people attractive, although that helps; rather it is some undefined social factor, some combination of confidence, warmth, popularity, and social skill, that makes people go ga-ga over you. Attractive people appear to like themselves, like new acquaintances, and seem to radiate "sexual warmth," that is, their own apparent interest in romantic involvement. This is not to say that people who are judged to be attractive are overtly seductive; they just seem to be people who are comfortable with themselves and comfortable with their own sexiness. Attractive people are like James Bond: They trust their attractiveness, and it this trust in their own attractiveness that helps people find them attractive.

These summary statements about what adults do and feel on average are, of course, just that: normative statements that do little or nothing to tell us about what particular people might find attractive or not. But it does appear that in the real, grown-up world, sexual confidence will win out just about every time. It doesn't matter what your SAT scores were, or whether you were once the treasurer of the Dungeons & Dragons Club. What matters is that you now radiate interest in romance and that you possess the complex skills required to communicate that interest.

Awkward people, on the other hand, radiate, well, awkwardness. On a recent installment of *Beauty and the Geek*, the so-called geeks, who are identified with a tag under their names at the beginning of every episode, like "Scooter: Harvard Graduate" or "Niels: Perfect SAT Scores," were given a challenge to exercise their pick-up skills. They were set loose in a public park with the instruction to get as many girls' phone numbers as possible. We can assume, of course, that socially skilled Harvard grads and smooth-talking SAT perfect-scorers were not chosen for this televised "reality" program, whose sole purpose is to reify existing nerd/geek stereotypes. But watching these awkward guys try to get phone numbers was painful indeed. The winner eventually hit upon the strategy of presenting himself as a loser: He told women he had been given a project to work on his self-esteem, and he needed as many phone numbers as he could get to boost himself up. Clever geek: He quickly figured out how to turn his disadvantage into an advantage. The other guys, even when provided with babe-magnet dogs as conversation starters, failed miserably. Awkwardness does appear to be a turnoff for a lot of average women and men.

This is not to say that nerdiness or geekiness is always a

romantic disadvantage among grown-ups. There is that segment of the adult population that fantasizes about geeks precisely because of their geekiness. This goes beyond the simple
effect of maturity: We know that, as adolescents turn into
adults, they grow out of these stereotypes and are willing to
consider romantic partners as real individuals. But there is also
that peculiar taste for awakening the unawakened that some
people find attractive. Adult nerds or geeks are sometimes
seen as interesting sexual partners because they are imagined
to be (a) unsophisticated and therefore (b) appreciative and
(c) inventive, but also (d) malleable, and most important, (e)
unable to compare you with any other lover because they have
had none. An example, from a British girl-blog, on why geeks
make good boyfriends: "Sex. Yep. Sex. I'm not really familiar
with this myself, but I've friends who've been intimate with
geek guys and it's raves all around. They say a virgin wrote the
Kama Sutra . . . all that time thinking about sex, imagining sex,
dreaming about sex (they are male after all), coupled with a
desire to make you happy? Use your imagination."

The romance author Vicki Lewis Thompson has made a
career of this sort of thing, writing popular novels with titles
like *Nerd in Shining Armor*, *Nerd Gone Wild*, and *The Nerd
Who Loved Me*. In each novel, the man initially thought to be
nerdy turns out to be, under his nerd exterior, a real stud.
These stories are fantasies about what it would be like to be a
Lois Lane who not only finds out her nerdy guy is Superman
but also actually turns him into Superman. It's the X-rated version of the "nerd-transcended" theme: The shy, awkward guy
becomes something else in the course of the book, and the sexy,
vibrant heroine has only herself to thank. But of course, like all

"nerd-transcended" stories, it depends on the existence of the stereotype for its vitality: If nerds stopped being so nerdy, they couldn't be rescued from their nerdiness by hot women with, as Thompson's advertising copy says, "a soft spot for nerds."

The adult story about the relationship between attractiveness and intelligence is, like most human behavior, pretty convoluted: There is no simple correlation, no simple story. So why, then, do we get the certitude on the way station to adulthood? Why are so many kids convinced, like Rennie (see chapter 1) that nerds are "smart, and they always get A's in school. But they're ugly, and they never, never get laid, 'cause no self-respecting girl would ever sleep with one of them." He's not getting this by observing the adults in his life: Even I, the nerdy-because-wearing-glasses psychologist interviewing him, am wearing a wedding ring. If it's not the propaganda, what data has he been observing that would make him believe this?

INTELLIGENCE: THE SECRET SHIELD

As it turns out, Rennie, like all the other kids who believe what he believes, that smart kids will never get laid, is onto something. He doesn't read adolescent health research, but there is some, and what it tells us is that Rennie is right, in a way. In 2000, a study titled "Smart Teens Don't Have Sex (or Kiss Much, Either)" appeared in the *Journal of Adolescent Health*. Lead author Carolyn Tucker Halpern carried out an analysis of a massive amount of data about children's behavior in the context of public health. Since early intercourse is defined in public health circles as a risk to adolescent health, she wanted to find out what demographic and behavioral factors were associated with the beginning of sexual activity of kids.

Halpern and her colleagues analyzed data from the National Longitudinal Study of Adolescent Health, an ongoing research project with a sample size of 12,000 kids from seventh through twelfth grades. She looked at another, smaller data set, of 300 girls who participated in the longitudinal Biosocial Factors in Adolescent Development study. Even after controlling for several other variables, including age, physical maturity, race, and the mother's education (as a rough estimate of social class), it was demonstrated that intelligence was significantly related to all different types of "partnered sexual activities" in which kids might participate. High IQ was closely related to the postponement of sexual activity. Interestingly, very low IQ was also associated with less sexual participation. Halpern discusses intelligence as a "protective factor" that helps kids stay out of the sexual marketplace for longer periods in adolescence.

We cannot assume, of course, that the nerd/geek stereotype is correct and that all or most smart kids are also socially awkward and therefore unable to find sex partners. This is patently untrue, despite what we see on *Beauty and the Geek*. As we have noted, "attractiveness," the province of the unawkward, is not significantly related to intelligence. So the reason for the smart kids to postpone sex cannot be because they are all "unattractive" in any objective sense. Any time spent on the campus of any selective private high school will also demonstrate to the casual observer that this is ridiculous: Kids at fancy prep schools, the schools you have to be really smart to get into, are just as vivacious, engaging, and attractive as any other adolescents. So Rennie's observation that smart kids don't get laid is partially confirmed by very solid research using huge samples of kids. It is true that smart kids have sex later than other kids. But the reason Rennie is right can't be the simple awkwardness factor. So what is it? Why might it be that, in Halpern's words, "smart teens don't have sex (or kiss much, either)"? Is the Seinfeld Axiom true after all? Does sex make you stupid?

HALOS AND RODENTS

Let's generate some hypotheses, just for fun. None of these hypotheses are currently "proven" because there are so many variables involved, and social-science research has not yet yielded any submerged treasure chest of Proven Facts. But one can generate several hypotheses about why smart kids postpone sexual activities, and since they are not mutually exclusive, they might all be partially true.

Nerd/geek stereotypes make smart kids seem less attractive. Halo effects work both ways, as we know. In adult research, having judged a stranger as "attractive" will make someone judge him or her to be more intelligent as well, because of what social scientists call the "Beautiful is good" effect. But, as we have seen, kids know one thing about nerds and geeks. The one thing they know for sure is the first thing

they learn about nerd and geeks, which is that they are undesirable. So if the first thing a kid knows about someone is that
he or she is smart or gets good grades, perhaps the reverse halo
effect sets in: The smart kid is then judged to be nerdy, awkward, socially unskilled, and unattractive, no matter what he
or she is objectively doing. In this sense, while "Beautiful is
good" might be true for adults, "good" (in the sense of smart
or successful in school) is not necessarily "beautiful," at least
for kids.

Extrapolating from laboratory research on attractiveness to
real social situations is always problematic anyway. In the laboratory, you don't know what you are supposed to think about
anyone. But kids' social reputations, as research tells us, are
highly resistant to change. Kids who have been awkward or
unskilled or weird in elementary school can have an undesirable reputation long after their objective behavior (as rated by
observers who do not know their reputations) has changed.
The comedian David Spade tells the story of his own experience in this regard. He tells of being rejected in junior high
school for being weird, while his older brother, in high school,
was one of the popular, cool kids. So when Spade went to high
school, he was immediately accepted as a cool kid because of
his older brother's "sponsorship," and his own age-mates were
furious. Spade is hilarious when describing how all his classmates went around saying, "Wait a minute, you've got this all
wrong. This kid's a jerk. He's not cool. He's never been cool."
But the high school kids didn't listen. They looked at the same
kid and instantly conferred a different halo, thanks to his older
brother.

So it might be that smart kids, no matter what they actually do, may not find partners because of the negative halo conferred by the nerd/geek stereotype. This implies that smart kids are seeking to engage in sexual activity as early as everyone else, but they aren't successful because other kids won't play along. As we shall see, there may be other reasons why smart kids don't seek "partnered sexual activity." But if they are seeking, they might not find.

This might be a good hypothesis, but Halpern's data do not bear it out. In fact, her research is pretty clear on this point. She considered this hypothesis, in a sense, by adding data on "physical attractiveness" and "personal attractiveness" into her predictive models. She found that these variables added a little predictive oomph: Kids who were smart *and* less physically or personally attractive started intercourse even later, but intelligence continued to be the strongest predictor, and the effect held up even when these other variables were controlled. So it probably isn't true that intelligence actually makes kids less attractive to others.

Young teenagers are fascists. The whole issue of "popularity" in middle school is a yawning gulf of misery for most people, at least when viewed in memory. That's because kids in middle school are, in a social sense, fascists. Conformity rises to a peak in kids roughly from the ages of tenth to thirteen, and desirability of all kinds is rigidly circumscribed by what is seen as "normal." The reasons for this are unclear, but it may have to do with puberty itself: The physical changes of puberty do not appear at the same time for all kids, and they are all in a state of suspended animation waiting for this to happen.

While they wait, and since they cannot impose any regularity on their bodies, they impose a rigid regularity on each other. Although this social hazing now starts earlier and earlier (see chapter 7), seventh grade is the peak. It is a time in most kids' lives when being different from the agreed-on norm is an absolute guarantee of social death.

In this sense, then, being smart would be a deal breaker for any kind of early initiation into "partnered sexual activity" because, earlier on, kids will shun anyone who is not normal. Being smart is just one condition that would exempt kids from the list of the attractive, just as any other condition would: being extremely tall or extremely diminutive, for example. This hypothesis would explain why the Halpern study found that the kids at either extreme end of the IQ continuum—kids with high IQs and kids with very low IQs—were both late bloomers sexwise. It would also explain why this effect goes away; after all, smart kids don't postpone sex forever, just for a little while. When kids get over their passion for normality (and by ninth grade this passion is definitely on the wane for most kids), intelligence ceases to be a liability, and smart kids are more likely to have kissing partners.

This hypothesis also requires, however, that kids who were at either end of the spectrum in terms of real interest to seventh-graders—being athletic, being funny, and being pretty—would also be sexual late starters. If it is just abnormality of any kind that is the turnoff, then kids who are outstanding athletes or outstanding beauties would be shunned along with the smart kids, and this does not appear to be the case, either from what we know in published research or from casual observation of middle schools. Middle school fascism is a real thing, but it alone does not adequately explain Halpern's findings. It must be something else.

Smart kids are closer to their parents. This might seem an obvious choice. Kids who get good grades might be seen as the kids who are generally more interested in pleasing grown-ups. This is, after all, an echo of the early versions of the nerd stereotype: for elementary school kids, the undesirable categories of "baby"—a person who needs adults too much—and "teacher's pet" or "suck-up"—the kid who wants to please adults too much—are inextricable from the nerd/geek stereotype. So kids who do well in school might be seen as part of the same tribe: kids who are more interested than their peers in following adults' rules. And if adults' rules include prohibitions on early sexual activity, it makes sense that the kids who care about adults' opinions of them might be sexual later starters.

Here's the problem with that simple version: Halpern is talking about smart kids, not kids who did well in school. Of course there's a big overlap, but the association Halpern notes in her research was that of *intelligence* and late sexual initiation, not school performance. Being intelligent is not the same thing as wanting to please adults; no amount of sucking up to adults is going to raise your IQ. In other studies published in the *Journal of Adolescent Health*, late sexual initiation has also been shown to be associated, not surprisingly, with religiosity. It seems to be true that kids who are encouraged by adults to resist sexual experimentation will end up having sex later than kids who are not so encouraged. So pleasing adults might also explain later sexual initiation, but it doesn't explain IQ as its own independent protective factor.

There is another, more complicated version of this that may get closer to the truth. Research in children's cognitive development has demonstrated for decades that kids who have more parental inputs in the course of growing up have higher measured intelligence. Studies have shown over and over that intelligence is not simply a God-given quality that unfolds over time in whatever amount you were given at birth. Kids who have more parental inputs—kids who have been copiously talked to, played with, and attended to by adults—end up having measurably higher IQs than kids who grow up with fewer such inputs. To put it another way: Kids who spend more time with adults as they are growing up have measurably higher IQs than kids who spend all their time with other kids. This explains, among other things, why oldest children have, on average, higher IQs than younger children in the same family.

We can assume, and observe in those we do observe, that this effect continues well into high school for close families. Parents who spend a lot of time with their kids don't drop them like hot potatoes when they reach puberty. Close families remain close: When they are teenagers, the kids in these close families still spend more time with adults, not as much as before, but more than their more peer-oriented peers. That means more adult supervision and more of a shared sense of values between adults and kids. So the statistical association between higher intelligence and later sexual activity might occur because both of these phenomena spring from the same source: lots of face time with parents. This is not to say that kids in these families don't like their peers or don't develop sexual interests at the same time as their peers. It is true, however, that there are a lot of kids who do not drop into the familiar oppositional stance of many American teenagers. There are kids who identify more closely with the adults in their lives and do not spend a lot of time trying to prove that adults are an alien and useless species. Some kids who are close with adults just identify with them more, with their interests and their values. And, unless these parents' values include pushing the kids into early sexual initiation, we might assume that these adult-identified kids are both more intelligent and less sexually experienced as a result.

The biology of the teen brain is part of the mix. This being a biological era in American mental health, we would be greatly remiss, and totally unhip, if we did not include a couple of purely biological hypotheses on our list when considering the Seinfeld Axiom. Thinking about the effects of parental involvement or halo effects is not nearly as sexy as thinking about the mysteries of the brain. Any consumer of popular culture has seen the pictures, those things that look like weirdly colored whales or old-fashioned circular maps of the world, the color-enhanced positron emission tomography (PET) scans that purport to show us what is really happening inside our brains. What they show is glucose metabolism, not actual thinking, but what the hell? We might as well go with the zeitgeist and see what we can come up with.

The teen brain has been much in the news, ever since the documentary on PBS, the cover story in *U.S. News & World*

Report, and the continuing news stories about adolescence itself as a mitigating condition in criminal sentencing. It turns out that recent brain-scanning technology has demonstrated that the frontal lobes, the last part of the brain to develop and the part most responsible for impulse control, are not fully developed by the time of sexual maturity. In fact, data from new scanning techniques show that the frontal lobes are not really fully mature, on average, until people are in their early twenties. We have always known, of course, that teenagers are impulsive, and developing sexual feelings just add more momentum to those felt urgencies. But the knowledge that the brain really is still preadult suggests that the impulsiveness of adolescence is not just a cultural artifact as some have claimed. Some in the legal profession are even using these new data to suggest that teenagers, even older teenagers, should not be held as criminally culpable as adults, even for capital crimes; their brain scans suggest that even when they are eighteen and beyond, young people just can't control themselves as well as adults.

In this version of Platonic psychology, the limbic system, seat of the sexual impulses or the brain's "reward centers," is one horse, and the frontal lobes are the other. But not all kids develop at the same rate. Might we postulate that kids whose frontal lobes are ahead of the game, so to speak, will have an advantage on intelligence testing as well as an enhanced ability to stop and think about sexual "partnered activity"? If we assume, as most developmental psychologists do, that the timetable for sexual maturity and the timetable for brain maturity can be different in each individual, we might expect that "smart" kids are those whose frontal lobes are developing earlier, or whose sexual maturity is happening later, or in whom there is some combination of developmental trajectories that keep the Platonic horses more evenly matched in terms of power.

The biggest problem with this hypothesis is that we just don't know yet. Brain research using the new tools of PET scans and functional magnetic resonance imaging (fMRI) is exploding, but it is far too early to be making broad statements about what we know about the effects of sexual maturity or differing developmental timetables on brain development. The portion of what is traditionally called "intelligence" contributed by frontal skills is small, so even if kids with earlier-developing frontal lobes are exercising more impulse control, the overall smartness conferred by their prodigious frontal lobes might be negligible, probably not enough for kids like Rennie to notice.

It's all in the prolactin. Finally, we can consider the most outlandish hypothesis of all: the purest, most biological version of the Seinfeld Axiom. It turns out that, at least for some lower mammals, sex really does make you stupid. Ten years ago, S. Marc Breedlove published a paper in *Nature* that showed that, for rats at least, the Seinfeld Axiom might hold true. Breedlove showed that rats who copulate have brains that are less developed, in terms of neuronal density, and that weigh less than the brains of rats prevented from copulating. Breedlove suggests that sexual activity may inscribe morphological changes on the developing brains of his rodent subjects. It is as if they are living out what every parent tells us: When they start thinking about sex, they stop thinking about anything else.

Could there be something on the neurochemical level that

produces the same effect in humans? Orgasm, after all, is a neurochemical event, and the mammalian body is bathed in several hormones, including oxytocin and prolactin, immediately after orgasm. Recent research on mammalian biology has demonstrated some dramatic behavioral effects of such hormone releases. This research is justly famous because of its implications for human experience: experiments with several mammals, such as monogamous prairie voles, have demonstrated the pair-bonding effect of some of these hormones by showing that creatures who have sex with each other are more likely to be pair-bonded and loyal to each other as a result of a release of neurotransmitters arising from orgasm. If these voles are experimentally prevented from having the anticipated postorgasmic neurotransmitter bath, they skip the pair-bonding. They don't experience mate loyalty after they mate.

If postorgasm hormones have such a dramatic effect on vole brains, what about human brains? Could there be something in the postorgasmic hormonal or neurotransmitter bath that has an effect on intelligence? Could all that oxytocin and prolactin really make us stupid? The obvious problem with this hypothesis, where developing teenagers are concerned, is the problem of masturbation: There are plenty of teenagers who are having orgasms but are not having "partnered sexual activity." So on the face of it, for this neurochemical hypothesis to be true, it would also have to be true that "smart teens don't have (solo) sex, either." If any or all orgasms somehow make people dumber, they would include what is tastefully called solo sex.

But wait. One of the chemicals that bathes the body after orgasm is prolactin, a hormone that has been suggested as having a role in the development of all kinds of mental phenomena, including various kinds of mental illness. And it turns out that prolactin, at least, is not fooled by solo sex. Normal humans show postorgasm levels of prolactin that are 400 percent higher after sexual intercourse than they are after masturbation. If regular prolactin baths somehow affect intelligence, or some component skills of intelligence, it might really be that sex makes you stupid, or at least stupider than you were before you started having it or stupider than you would have been if you held off for a few years. Of course, it could turn out that, in fact, regular prolactin baths make you smarter—a finding that would be greeted warmly by adolescents everywhere. ("C'mon, Mom, lighten up. We're just trying to get into Harvard here. . . .") Or it could be that prolactin baths have no effect at all on the developing brain. The point is, research on the effects of neurotransmitters on brain development is in its infancy. While that jury is out, we will have to rely on old-fashioned developmental psychology for recommendations.

All of these hypotheses may turn out to be true or partially true, but whatever the factual status of the invisible shield that intelligence provides, it is clear that the relationship of intelligence to sexual activity is a lot more complicated than nerd/geek stereotypes suggest. Adults all know this, but adults are much more able to follow their hearts wherever they lead. What kids "know" is what matters here, and what kids "know" is that nerds and geeks don't have sex, because no self-respecting person would have sex with them. If this protects nerds and geeks from the deleterious effects of too-early intercourse, the stereotypes turn out to be a good thing. But the desexualization of nerd-labeled kids also has an effect on the labelers: It's just another reason to avoid any and all of the nerd stigmas. Unfortunately for some kids, they then act according to the Seinfeld Corollary: Since smartness is a turnoff, stupidity is a turn-on. As we shall see, the Seinfeld corollary is only one of the many reasons why being nerdy is a lot better for kids than it first appears.

6.

THE GEEK SQUAD

· OR ·

WHY YOU'RE NOT GRATEFUL TO THE GUY WHO FIXES YOUR COMPUTER

Consider, if you will, the case of Bill, a man in his late fifties. His kids have grown up and moved out of the house. It is February, and it's the weekend, and it's too cold to be out doing chores around the yard or cleaning the garage. But he wouldn't really be doing that anyway; he's in the house getting ready for spring. Spring comes in early May, but he needs to be ready. He is engrossed in his notebooks from last spring, looking at drawings of bugs he made in his logbook or looking at the bodies of bugs he collected, bodies that are now in little plastic boxes on his desk. He is consulting his sizable library of books about freshwater entomology, and he is slowly, carefully reproducing those bugs with feathers and pieces of colored string. He's making trout flies, getting ready to go back to the same streams where he caught the bugs, only this time armed with little handmade replicas with barbless hooks, so he can catch (and release) the trout that ate the bugs last year at this time. He has a lot of knowledge about trout flies and many opinions, and he can sometimes express his opinions strongly when evaluating the quality of another fly-tier's product.

Quiz question 1: Is he a nerd? Question 2: Is he a geek?

Now consider the case of Andrew. He's twenty-seven years old, and he lives with his roommates in a big city. He works as a salesclerk at Best Buy, advising people about which television they should buy. (Lately, he's been caught up in questions about high-definition-television specs.) Evenings and weekends, when he is not out with his girlfriend, he watches old episodes of *Star Trek*, and he has a lot of the dialogue from these episodes memorized. He also participates in online fan fiction forums where people write new episodes for the old *Star Trek* characters and people comment on the quality of each other's fan fiction. He has strong opinions on whether the original *Star Trek* was better than *Star Trek: The Next Generation*, and he sometimes gets disagreeable with others, online and in person, when expressing these opinions.

Quiz question 3: Is Andrew a nerd? Question 4: Is he a geek?

Let's see how you did. The correct answers are: questions 1 and 3, no; questions 3 and 4, yes. If you answered correctly, you are a well-socialized American consumer of popular culture. If not, you really haven't been paying attention, or you have spent the last ten years working overseas. How do we know? Well, let's go to the data. A quick check (performed in August 2010) using a simple Google search as a score generator yielded the following number of hits for terms used to described aficionados of fly fishing:

"Fly-fishing nerd": 5 hits
"Fly-fishing geek": 2,940 hits
"Star Trek nerds": 622,000 hits
"Star Trek geeks": 627,000 hits

The reasons for this are not so obvious, at least to me. We know from nerd and geek self-tests that nerds and geeks possess arcane knowledge that few other people possess. If you ever watched the late, unlamented television show *Beat the Geeks* you know this as well. In that show, which aired from the fall of 2001 until its demise in the fall of 2002, the term "geek" was just a synonym for "expert." The show featured the Movie Geek, who knew everything about movies; the Music Geek, who knew everything about music; and the TV Geek, who knew everything about old television shows. In some ways, *Beat the Geeks* was wonderfully instructive about the role of expertise in popular culture: These guys were just guys who knew a lot of stuff, but they had odd gownlike costumes like wizards, spoke in bizarre oracular tones, and had weird haircuts and facial hair, as if, in the archetypal universe of popular culture, expertise was just one shade off from wizardry, or psychosis, or both.

But fly-fishing experts are not called nerds (except by 5 people in the whole world, which doesn't really count), and fly fishermen are rarely called fly-fishing geeks, although the knowledge they possess is certainly arcane: There are really very few people in the world who can tell the difference between *Cinygmula mimus* and *Cinygmula tarda*, much less make replicas of them. So it is not simply the mastery of arcane knowledge that gets someone called a nerd or geek; otherwise, Bill would be so called.

Consider (just once more, I promise) the fly fisherman. If he is a socially skilled fly fisherman, we would observe that he will not overwhelm non–fly fisherman with his knowledge of the life cycle of mayflies. He will figure out who is interested and who is probably not, and he will act accordingly. If Bill is not a socially skilled person, he will bore people to tears with his perorations on mayflies, in which case we would call him a bore. But even if he *is* a bore, it still doesn't make him a geek. If one of the stigmas of the dyed-in-the-wool nerd or geek is the inability to know who is interested and who is not interested in one's own peculiar passions (the sick Asperger-ish nerd we met in chapter 4), this inability should be content-neutral. Bores can be boring on any topic if they fail to notice you're not interested.

But it's the deep interest in *particular* subjects that merits the label "nerd" or "geek." It is here we have to consider what it is about interest in science and technology that makes people so eager to apply the nerd/geek stereotype. What is it about interest in technology that gets people labeled with such a pejorative term? Why does a passion for things technological, like computers or chemistry or mathematics, merit the "nerd" label, whereas a passion for other, equally arcane things does not merit the label? To look into this is to look into the weird core of American self-destructiveness: Why is it that the very people who are practically ensured to succeed in the twenty-first century—science and technology workers—need to be labeled as ugly, scary, unattractive, or repulsive while everyone else gets a free pass?

THE WAY THINGS WORK:
FIXING AND DRIVING THE CAR

An older friend of mine laughs when she tells the story about her grandmother learning to drive. Her grandfather was not at all in favor of this project. When his young wife announced she planned to learn to drive the family car, he said, "Mary, you don't understand. That's a *machine* we're talking about." Implicit in her grandfather's statement (in addition to the obvious sexism) was the notion that being able to drive a car went along with some knowledge about how to repair a car: Knowing how to drive meant knowing how to fix the machine when something went wrong with it.

It was not so long ago that this attitude prevailed in America: Using something machinelike, whether it was a bicycle, a lawn mower, or a car, implied mastering the ability to repair it as well. In part this was a necessity born of rural isolation. It is probably still true that farmers are the best nonprofessional mechanics. But as more people like my friend's grandmother began to drive, people began to depend on professional mechanics to help out when the car ceased to operate. Driving, or using a wide variety of other machines, no longer implied a knowledge of or interest in the workings of the machines or how to repair them.

But amateurs could still be interested in mechanics. Those of us who grew up in simpler times remember when a lot of high school boys took an interest in souping up their cars; spending time taking apart cars was something boys frequently did together. Kids who were interested in cars had their own social niche and reputation—there was always that thing about people who were "getting their hands dirty"—but interest in things mechanical, in *how things work,* was not seen as weird or unusual or antisocial. Indeed there are certainly a number of iconic images—visual stereotypes, as it were—of auto mechanics that portray them as masculine, self-assured, and sexy. In the fifties, or in movies or television shows set in the fifties, we had James Dean in *Rebel Without a Cause* or John Travolta and his friends in *Grease,* and today we have the *Fast and the Furious* movies, all of which feature mechanically inclined men who also get all the hot girls.

So what happened? Why did, and do, we have images of mechanically inclined men who get girls, while technologically inclined men get none of the girls? Why do kids now grow up believing that knowing, and being interested in, how things work is weird and undesirable? When did this change? Although no one can know the answer precisely, we can imagine research that might answer the question. We might conduct research that looks at groups of really old people and then groups of successively younger people to see if their attitudes and stereotypes about the mechanically and technologically inclined really have changed. No one seems to have done this research, and even if they had, we still wouldn't be able to explain the change. We can only hazard some guesses.

One reason might be the lack of sexy visual iconography for current technological work. In my work with children and with college students, I am constantly amazed at the power of the accumulated visual images they have and how those visual images affect their concepts, their worldview, and their theorizing. Those who were educated in college before the 1980s might be amazed, if they haven't seen any entry-level college textbooks recently, at how visual these books are: They are loaded with eye-popping graphic displays of every kind. Entry-level textbooks without the graphics are an extremely hard sell, as are entry-level courses without the DVDs. And the visual images, the icons kids live with, have an enormous and, to an older generation's eyes, irrational effect on knowledge acquisition. When I ask my brand-new college students to write down, on the first day of class, everything they know about Sigmund Freud, the thing they say most often is that he was "an old man with a cigar." In other words, a lot of what they know comes from seeing the iconic photos of Freud in his older years. But more important, what they go on to say is clearly affected by their visual image of Freud. His "oldness" affects almost every subsequent thought: He was cranky, intransigent, senile, and disapproving, as the necessary correlates of "oldness." Freud's entire life's work is discredited in the mind of these students, because he was "old." When I pass around a picture of the young Freud, a handsome man with black hair and a black beard (a picture of Freud from about the time he was writing *The Interpretation of Dreams*), they are amazed, as if it had never occurred to them that old people were once young. And although the black-haired picture doesn't immediately change uninformed but rabid anti-Freudians into Freudians (which is not my project in any case), it does go some distance toward getting college students to give Freud a fair hearing. As the old man might have said if he were living in the year 2010, iconography is destiny.

So a simple answer to the problem of tech man and his cultural icon is that it is difficult to portray or show a romantic picture of what technology workers do. "Fly fisherman" doesn't conjure an image of a middle-aged man poring over entomology books with his reading glasses perched on his nose; it conjures Brad Pitt in *A River Runs Through It*, a handsome man flicking his fishing rod into a pristine river with majestic mountains looming in the background. There is not much that is rugged, or heroic-*appearing*, in what tech workers do. They sit and look at computer screens. This is why, in the old days, there were very few movies featuring the heroic adventures of accountants. And this is why, in the new days, the visual iconography of technology workers is always spruced up with snazzy graphic imagery. The movie *A Beautiful Mind*, in which the mathematician hero went crazy (what else would you expect from a mathematician?), solved the dramatic problem by having numbers and formulas appear shimmering in the near and middle distance. The television series *Numb3rs*, about a heroic crime-fighting math genius, solves the problem the same way, with snazzy graphic displays of what the genius is thinking. It is as if the image is saying, "Well, he doesn't jump around too much, but his thoughts do! Look at those numbers dance!" It remains to be seen whether a show like *Numb3rs* can stay on the air, but at least it attempts to solve one problem by making math look heroic and even kind of hot.

It may be true that part of the current ickiness of the nerd/geek stereotype flows from an inherent problem in how to portray in an arresting visual way the excitement of technological work to a younger generation for whom visual iconography is so important. But this is far from the whole story. Another part of the story is the rage lying just below the surface of the apparent goofy humor of nerd/geek stereotyping. The portrayals of nerds and geeks as repulsive and creepy is in part an expression of real anger about the shape of the future and about the loss of a vital piece of the American past. As a clinician, I know that rage is an emotion felt and expressed by individuals; speculating about collective rage is, well, speculative, because it is difficult to know who it is that is angry. But collective rage is real: The outpouring of real rage in thousands or millions of individual Muslims around the world in 2006 was real, in that it was really felt in all those individual people when the right button was pushed—in this case, the button being cartoons satirizing the prophet Mohammed. The rage fueling the nerd/geek stereotype is quieter rage, but it is still rage, and when one sees the virulence and nastiness of middle school kids picking on nerds or geeks, *rage* does not seem to be too strong a term. It's collective rage because a button has been pushed in thousands, or millions, of American breasts. But what's the button?

THE WAY THINGS DON'T WORK

Let's go back for a moment to Jefferson and Jackson. Let's go back to Ichabod Crane and Brom Bones. As we saw, the iconography of our early history, presented in popular literature like "The Legend of Sleepy Hollow" and in high-flown academic literature like Emerson's "The American Scholar," presented us with a dichotomous choice: the Man of Action versus the Man of Reflection. The Man of Action was American, independent of mind, and masculine as opposed to the Man of Reflection, who was characterized as European, dependent on book-learning, and effete. In this mythological world, it was the Man of Action who could "get things done." Indeed, being practical, knowing how to do things, was the special province of the American. The American invented things, useful things, instead of reading about antique, desiccated things.

But the Man of Action's claim to superiority over the Man of Reflection was his mastery of the practical. The romance of the American inventor was, for two hundred years, the romance of the mechanic, the tinkerer. Benjamin Franklin didn't have to go to school to figure out bifocals or the Franklin stove; he just needed to see a need and then figure out in his workshop how to meet it. Thomas Edison and the Wright brothers might be the last such American inventors whom we can still romanticize as tinkerers, people just like you and me, only luckier, who happened to figure out something necessary in their spare time and make a huge fortune when it changed American life.*

But the products and processes that now change American life are not invented by tinkerers. *Time* magazine's list of best inventions for the year 2006 includes the following: a robot that can rescue wounded soldiers on the battlefield; a power saw that features a sensor that can detect an impending collision with human flesh and stop the saw from rotating before it

---

*The explicit connection between the American tinkerer and the American myth was trotted out again as recently as July 2007, when *The New York Times Magazine* celebrated the Fourth of July with Jack Hitt's article about NASA's turning to tinkerers to solve problems that their own engineers have been unable to solve. The tinkerers were charming, but their success rates have been less than stellar so far. The romance of the American tinkerer endures, mostly in the fantasy lives of the tinkerers themselves.

cuts off a finger; a scanner that can detect blood-alcohol levels by scanning the surface of the skin; and YouTube, the video-clip website that has changed the course of moviemaking as well as politics. Of all the inventions listed, the only one that could have been invented by a tinkerer is the shirt that, when placed on the body, simulates a human hug . . . sort of like a straitjacket only cuddly. While it is kind of cute in a peculiar, Temple Grandin way, the hug shirt is not likely to change the way we live as YouTube has already done, and as the battle robot and the blood-alcohol scanner might in the near future. These things were not invented by tinkerers; they were invented by people who had, and have, extremely sophisticated technological and computer skills at their disposal. These things were invented or developed by people who went to school, studied math and programming and chemistry, did their homework, and also delighted in figuring out new ways to do things.

So why should we be so mad at them? Why the rage? Well, speaking of tinkerers, have you talked to any car mechanics lately? Car mechanics, at least the ones I know, fall into three camps: the ones who curse the day the computer was ever invented, because they have to spend all their time reprogramming or resetting faulty sensors and computer-driven car parts; the ones who have come to accept, if not like, the necessity for spending much more time pushing buttons than they do turning wrenches; and the ones who only work on old, precomputerized cars because they love being *mechanics*. It is the same with mechanics of all kinds. In my neck of the woods, mill workers who used to have jobs that required mostly physical strength and reliability have mostly been replaced by people who can run and troubleshoot automated production lines, and they're not happy about it. The sheer pleasure of taking apart a machine, diagnosing its difficulties, and putting it back together, something that naturally talented mechanics can do almost from the day they are born, is a thing of the past, except in the case of "antique" machines. And whom do these guys blame when they feel useless or dispossessed? Guess who?

Yep. The geeks who are "taking over the world." When we look at all the sources of the virulence of negative nerd and geek stereotyping in kids, we must, of course, look to all the messages coming from the adult world. In addition to the messages kids get from the adult-controlled media culture, however, there are the more direct and personal messages about economic displacement coming from individual parents who feel resentful about their old ways of knowing being supplanted. Even parents who are keeping up with changing technologies need to be constantly retrained, and their grousing does not fall on deaf ears. The situation is not unlike that of kids whose parents are freaking out about outsourcing, kids whose brutal racism is an act of filial piety. Many of the most antinerd kids are kids whose parents are constantly anxious about their ability to keep up with more and more sophisticated workplace demands. Even if the kids themselves are tech-savvy, and their tech-beleaguered parents want them to be tech-savvy, the kids' nerd-bashing persists as a way of avenging the family honor.

Of course, this nerd-bashing is not limited to mechanics. White-collar workers of all kinds are just as resentful about geeks taking over the world. Steve Kroft, in his *60 Minutes* television story about the Geek Squad service company, can chortle in his avuncular way about the irony of the fact that our technology "has become so complicated to set up, program, and fix, that most of us don't know how to do it, giving rise to a multibillion-dollar service industry populated by the very people who used to be shunned in the high school cafeteria: geeks." But he doesn't consider that our children might hear us bitching about how much we hate to have to depend on technical-support geeks, and so our children will obediently refuse to sit with their geeky counterparts in the high school cafeteria. It's really not as ironic as Kroft supposes; it's much more literal and direct. And so even when the kids' nerd-bashing is incredibly vicious, it is not actively discouraged by many contemporary parents. The sense that the "nerds are taking over the world" is as pervasive among tech-challenged people as the feeling that nerds or geeks deserve punishment because they are *taking* something that used to belong to their historic counterparts: They are reaching across the historical Man of Action–Man of Reflection divide and stealing "practical effects on the world at large" for their own team. That alone is worthy of punishment. And since you can't punish the real, grown-up nerds and geeks in the adult workplace, you can let your kids punish their kids.

But nerd-bashing is allowed also because if "nerds are taking over the world," they will be compensated in the future. The Bill Gates biography has inspired millions of nonnerdy parents and kids to pick on nerds because . . . Wait a minute—how does this work? Oh, yeah. Making them miserable now is fair play, because they will end up to be billionaires later anyway. This is the logic behind the story lines of movies like *Romy and Michelle's High School Reunion*, in which the former nerd appears in his private helicopter and rescues the former outcast girls from humiliation at their reunion and from professional failure ever after. Of course, it is not at all logical: From a moral point of view, dishing out cruelty now because the recipient of that cruelty will get rewarded later on by somebody else doesn't make any sense. It is also not logical from a practical point of view, since having friends from high school who remember you fondly when they are billionaires may come in handy. But, like any action based primarily on envy, nerd-bashing is never logical.

A PASSION FOR PRECISION

The fact of the matter is that, if they don't commit suicide because of the merciless way they are treated, kids who are truly talented and studious in science and technology probably will end up just fine. But as we have seen in chapter 3, it is the effect of nerd and geek prejudices on the vast middle that should be of greater concern. What can we do for kids who could do well in science and math or computer programming, or well enough, but are subtly and not-so-subtly discouraged from doing so by negative stereotyping? They are the ones that need help in the short run, so that they can thrive in the long run.

I put this question to Esther Dyson, the author of *Release 2.0: A Design for Living in the Digital Age* and one of America's leading authorities on emerging technologies and emerging markets, intellectual property, and the control and organization of the Internet. Dyson has a childhood history that would seem to suggest a fair amount of high school nerdity, although she reports she was never particularly bothered by high school labels. "I suppose I was kind of wonky," she says. "But it never bothered me. I grew up at the Institute for Advanced Study at Princeton, so I was surrounded by other kids more or less like me." She went off to boarding school in Britain, then to a program for gifted and talented high school students at Telluride. She then went on to early admission to Harvard and never looked back.

Dyson never let the stereotyping by others affect her in the least, but she is concerned about the lack of engagement with science and technology among children today, and she sees it as getting worse, not better. "Kids have a natural interest in how things work, but somewhere along the line we fail at fostering that natural interest," she says. She suggests there is a missing link in early science education, when we might take kids' natural interest in how things work and expand that interest to teach kids how the things they care about—subways, computers, and televisions, for example—actually operate. In this, she enunciates a well-articulated principle of progressive education: Teach kids about things in which they have a natural interest, not about things that are meaningless abstractions. But she suggests that we extend that principle even further and even younger to help kids of all kinds, not just kids with a talent for math or science, to feel passionately interested in scientific endeavor.

This is a wonderful idea, but it requires a great deal from teachers of elementary school children. It requires that elementary school teachers find in themselves, and then inspire in their students, a passion for precision. Because making things work—taking them apart and putting them back together so that they work or making new things that work—requires precision. It requires getting answers that are right, not just sort of right, because machines won't work if the instructions and parts are assembled in a sort-of-right fashion. It is just this passion for precision that gets many kids stuck with the nerd label.

If you observe the nerd-labeled people you know, many of them will demonstrate a passion for precision, a deep satisfaction in getting answers exactly right. Kids who are extremely talented in math will demonstrate very early on an almost aesthetic pleasure in seeing patterns, predicting answers to problems, and seeing their predictions come true. These are the kids who delight in knowing the value of *pi* to as many digits as they can remember. (And indeed, knowing the value of *pi* to more than three digits is a staple of nerd self-tests; if this sort of thing turns you on, your score goes way, way up.) These are the kids who discover patterns in numbers and find genuine delight in them. They dig it when they figure out that the digits in any multiple of 9, when added, will add up to 9 or a multiple of 9. They put themselves to sleep at night by adding sequences of numbers, but then have to get up out of bed to check if their answers are right. And don't get them started on prime numbers or perfect squares.

This kind of passion for precision can certainly seem, to people who do not have it, as either a great talent or an illness, or both. In my consulting work with parents, I frequently run across this ambivalence: Parents want their kids to succeed but don't want them to have the passion or talent that might lead to success but that also might make them seem geeky (or

"Aspergy" or, God forbid, "anal"). Take the example of Marcy, the mother of a ninth-grader who was consulting me about her son's school progress. She was bemoaning Tim's grades in science and math, and trying to justify him to his teachers and to me. "It's not like he doesn't work hard, because he does. He works really hard, but it's hard for him to do well in science."

"Why is that? Is science particularly hard?" I say, thinking he's not getting along with his science teacher.

"Yeah. I mean, he's not a geek, so it's really hard for him."

Wait a minute. Now I'm getting confused. "I don't get it," I say, trying to sound curious but disinterested. "Is there something he's lacking that makes science hard for him?"

"Well, you know, he's not one of those kids who likes getting the right answers. I mean, he likes getting the answers right, but he doesn't *enjoy* it the way some kids enjoy it."

"Can you give me an example?" I say, less patiently than I should.

"Like that kid Artie in his class. You know him, the really geeky kid who's always on the high honor roll? Artie likes right answers; it really matters to him if he understands a formula. But Timmie doesn't care that much. He doesn't feel excited about science, so it's twice as hard for him. I mean, he doesn't get all goofy about chlorine molecules or whatever it is. *He's not a geek*. And we're happy about that. But it does put him at kind of a disadvantage."

This is one of those moments when I want to call those alien visitors back. "Listen to this," I want to say. "Did you hear what she said? What do you make of that?" Marcy loves her son, and she wants to help. But she is saying something that is really very peculiar. She seems to be saying, "I am happy he doesn't have that condition we call geekiness, but not having that condition, as unacceptable as it is, does put our son at a competitive disadvantage in school." She's one step away from saying, "Isn't there a way we could get him to like getting right answers without being a geek?" or maybe "It's not fair that geeks, whom we all agree are undeserving, get to have this unfair advantage that makes school easy for them."

What she is saying is clear enough in a way. It would not be that different from saying that if all the kids were *required* to play band instruments, the musically talented kids have a leg up, because they have a talent for music. But what is peculiar is the labeling of something so general—"enjoying getting answers right"—as a special or unusual talent that is also a little unsavory. It's as if she were saying Artie is cheating because he has that passion for precision that her son lacks, and she also seems to be saying that, since her son lacks this passion, he will never have it, and he will always find it hard to get right answers because right answers don't turn him on. Unfortunately, it looks like Timmie is going to have a hard slog ahead of him in life, unless he finds a career that does not require precision, or right answers, very often.

GEEKS: BORN AND NOT MADE?

This attitude, that a passion for precision is born and not made, gets close to the beating heart of the perceived geek/technology romance. For people who enjoy precision, science and mathematics can be truly enjoyable, although a poet, graphic artist, violinist, or furniture maker can express a passion for precision just as readily. But for people who don't enjoy precision, the temptation is always there to pathologize people who do. If it's not Asperger's syndrome (see chapter 4), then it's something else, some kind of neurosis that contemporary teens express when they use the word "anal." As a great admirer of Freud, it always makes me chuckle to hear kids bat this word around as casually as they do with really no idea of what it means to be "anal." When my psychology students hear the classic Freudian explanation of obsessive or compulsive defenses as, primarily, defenses against coprophilia, they think I must be kidding. "That's not what 'anal' means, is it?" they say, usually in horror. "Yep," I say, trying as usual to be deliberately provocative. "Better keep lining up your shoes and washing your hands, because if you stop, you never know what you'll end up playing with." They know I'm kidding, but I'm only partially kidding. I'm not kidding when I tell them that the term "anal" should be reserved for people with truly severe, psychogenic emotional difficulties, not for people who like to spell things correctly. Indeed, the term is very often applied to me when I insist that my students use standard English spelling in all their written work; after all, they all live in an e-mail and instant-messaging and text-messaging environment where nonstandard spelling is the rule because standard spelling takes too long. To them, I am impossibly "anal," just another way of saying that people who enjoy, or insist on, precision are somehow twisted.

If a passion for precision, or a delight in getting details

right, derives from an illness, say Asperger's syndrome, or from a neurosis, say obsessive-compulsive disorder, then Marcy's complaint about her son would make sense. If a passion for precision is so pathological, who would want it? It becomes another, only very slightly milder, version of the talents of autistic savants. Yes, you might want a memory for facts and figures, but do you have to be the Rain Man to get it? On second thought, no, thanks. I'll just have to slog along, working harder than I should have to work, because I wasn't born geeky.

Indeed, this is the one thing that teachers and parents hear children say more than any other thing they ever say about math: "Math is so harrrd." Since I am not a teacher, I don't have to hear it as much as they do. But if I did have to hear it that much, that word, "harrrd," delivered in that whiny tone kids use when they are complaining about something they want deliverance from, I would sooner or later put out my ears the way Oedipus put out his eyes when he just couldn't take it anymore. Observing this from a historical distance, the reported experience of math as way too "harrrd" is also kind of mysterious. Since when did this happen? Since when did a normal and ordinary adult expectation for kids, like algebra class, turn into a little spin on the Catherine wheel? When did the normative expectation of how difficult things ought to be change so dramatically? It might be impossible to understand when kids' feeling about what was normally expected of them went south or when math and science became "harrrder" than reading and writing. But thinking about this developmentally and linguistically, we might come to understand a little more about why. It might be a matter of how we talk about math and science.

THE POETRY OF THE PRECISE

When we talk about math or science being hard, it implies, of course, an opposite: "Harrrd" is always stated with an implicit contradistinction to something that is less so—something easier, or softer, or something. "Harrrd" is, after all, a metaphoric term that suggests the operation of what linguists and cognitive psychologists and philosophers of language call a metaphorical entailment. Metaphorical entailments made their debut in 1980 with the publication of the groundbreaking book *Metaphors We Live By* by George Lakoff and Mark Johnson. Simply put, metaphorical entailments are systems of thought, or ways of thinking about things in commonsensical terms, that are generated by the metaphorical terms we use in everyday speech. Lakoff has since extended his work to the area of politics, trying to explicate the Republican Party's ascendancy in the late 1990s with reference to the GOP's mastery of metaphor. For example, he dissects the term "tax relief," which has been used in a disciplined fashion by conservatives since the first days of the Bush administration. "Tax relief," Lakoff argues, is not a neutral term; it implies that there is an affliction, "taxes" from which people need relief. But there are other ways of framing taxes, such as "paying one's dues," a metaphor suggesting that taxes are the price of membership in a free society and that everyone must pay one's dues. But consistently using the term "tax relief" and getting it into the mainstream changes the commonsense notion of the essence of taxes, and moves it in the desired direction (from a conservative point of view).

Lakoff's work has been extended to the world of science and mathematics in a paper by a scholar who studies, oddly enough, the interface between literature and psychology. In his 2000 paper "Cold Hard World \ Warm Soft Mommy," Burton Melnick tackles the metaphoric entailments of some of our earliest categorical distinctions. Melnick begins with the metaphorical distinction made in our spoken language between things that are described as cold and hard and things that are described as warm and soft. He then goes on to describe the qualities, the metaphorical entailments, that form this particular system. His tabulation reads, in part:

COLD/HARD	WARM/SOFT
Solid	Liquid or gaseous
Uncomfortable	Comfortable
Unsympathizing	Sympathetic
Reliable	Mutable
Well-defined	Ill-defined
Comprehensible in detail	Not comprehensible in detail
Sharp (sometimes blunt)	Flaccid or spongy
Precise	Imprecise
Difficult	Easy

It is those last two, of course, that should give us pause. If Melnick is correct, the earliest metaphoric entailments make a distinction between the human world, the "warm" world of mommies, and the physical world, the "cold" world of hard, cold facts. In this metaphorical system, precision is always hard in both senses of the word: Precision is unyielding and well defined, but precision is also "harrrd." It is, by its metaphorical nature, difficult. The idea that precision could be fun, enlivening, or exhilarating is swimming against the tide: the language system that tells us that precision is, in its essence, inhuman.

It is precisely this feature of our current linguistic currency that alarms technophiles who worry about Americans' increasing disengagement with technology. Esther Dyson gives voice to this concern when she speaks to the problem of getting kids engaged with technology. She notes that technology itself as well as the people who understand it and use it are seen by nontechies as somehow inhuman. How can it be that technology, arguably the most human of endeavors, is now seen as inhuman *in its essence*? How is it that, in this country at least, the hardness of technology is such a barrier to kids who might want to use it or understand it but who don't want to be dehumanized?

Melnick's proposition is testable, although it has not yet been rigorously tested. We could examine the linguistic history of phrases such as "hard sciences" and see if there is some correlation between the use of such metaphoric phrases and disengagement of the general public from the world of science. We could examine the linguistic systems of countries that are beating the pants off us in terms of science education and see if our unhelpful metaphorical entailments exist in their languages. If Melnick's observations turn out to be true, at least we will know what we're up against: a culture that indoctrinates children from the cradle to believe that precision is a world of pain to be overcome, not a world of comfort, warmth, or human interaction.

WARM, SOFT ARITHMETIC

At the very least, Melnick's thought-provoking contribution to the study of language suggests something of how we should be teaching our children. If we teach children that precision is hard, we shouldn't be surprised when they complain later that it is "harrrd." We might rethink educational techniques that emphasize warm flow first and gelid precision later. The "free write" technique so popular in my own college students' high school educations is a case in point: They are encouraged to get the flow of ideas going by writing a formless outpouring of ideas and associations first and making it precise later. The precision is like medicine, the unpleasant dram that will turn freedom into readable prose. Unfortunately, as many current college students painfully demonstrate, the medicine is hard to take; the prose never quite reaches the readable stage because it is, from its inception, disorganized. Imposing precision after the fact, while not an inherently bad idea, often doesn't work. But one reason it doesn't work is that precision is felt to be alien, unwarm, and unfree. The whole idea of the free write reifies the idea that precision is too "hard," or "harrrd."

The nerd/geek stereotype assumes, in its very essence, that nerds and geeks, those who are "born to" a passion for precision, are somehow inhuman or sick. But of course Melnick's work suggests an alternative explanation: Nerd-labeled kids are those who have not had the indoctrination about the "cold hard world" and the "warm soft mommy." These may be kids who have been lucky enough to feel nurtured by precision, by exactitude, by detail, the ones who have a warm, soft mommy (or daddy) whose favorite exciting thing to do with them is not to cuddle up and make up stories but to look things up in a dictionary, read the encyclopedia, or construct a machine and make it work. The degree of brainwashing to which we have been subjected by our metaphoric entailments is apparent when we think about the unlikeliness of this picture. But it is not impossible; it happens all the time in nerd-labeled families. Perhaps we have come to a time in human history when, as teachers and as parents, we need to find a way to erase the distinction between the "cold hard world" and the "warm soft mommy" once and for all, and impart the warmth and humanity of precision and technology to our children.

7.

THEY'RE NOT UGLY, THEY JUST NEED A MAKEOVER

· OR ·

WHY THEY THINK NO ONE CAN SEE THE TAPE ON THEIR GLASSES

Marty is nine years old. She's a cute fourth-grader with lots of friends, and she does well in school. She plays soccer after school like all the other kids, and she's starting flute lessons because her parents are musical and she appears to be musical as well. She is pretty happy—not, her parents think, the kind of kid who would ever need to see a child therapist. But all of a sudden she is getting headaches and stomachaches, every Sunday night. By Monday morning, she seems desperately ill. She clutches her belly and moans so convincingly that her parents have had her to the pediatrician twice and have set her up to see a gastroenterologist before they notice the obvious: She gets better every weekend and gets sick again, but only on Sunday nights. So they bring her to me.

We talk a little with Mom and Dad, and then without. Marty is articulate, accomplished, and seemingly without a care in the world. Has something happened at school, I ask, that has made her uncomfortable there? Nope. Not a thing. Everything is fine at school; in fact, she says, she is missing too much of it and feels a little worried about falling behind. I go back through my mental checklist. No history of separation difficulties. No sudden illnesses or crises with other family members. No history of any unreasonable fears. Nothing. So, in quiet desperation, I call her folks back in and go back through her recent medical history. No long illnesses, no surgeries. No exposure to movies about death or dying. Anything else, anything, that has affected her schoolwork? Nope. We're all stumped. Finally her mom muses, "Well, she did have those headaches for a little while earlier in the fall, and we realized she couldn't see the blackboard as well as she should. So then she got her glasses, and everything was just fine."

I look over at Marty, who is sporting a very understated, simple, fashionable (for a nine-year-old) pair of wire-rimmed glasses. She has that "Don't ask me about this, don't, don't, please don't" look that one comes to recognize when one is a child therapist. So, all together, we talk a little longer. I notice that Mom and Dad are also wearing glasses that are somewhat less fashionable than Marty's but not particularly remarkable. Then, as soon as I can, I send Mom and Dad back out to the waiting room.

"So," I say, trying for that avuncular tone that always worked so well for Fred Rogers. "You got the glasses recently?" Marty is a good kid, open and trusting with adults, and she doesn't lie particularly well. When I ask about the glasses, tears well up in her eyes. "What happened?"

"There's this girl in my class, Lisa," she says. "She really started making fun of me when I got my glasses. She started calling me a nerd, and pretty soon all the boys started calling me that, too."

"So . . . what did she mean? What is a nerd, anyway?"

"I don't know. I mean, I thought I knew. But I didn't think I was one."

"So are you one?"

"I don't know. What if I am?"

"Let's figure out first what we're talking about. What is a nerd, anyway?"

"Like a human computer. Someone nobody likes. Someone who has no friends and just sits at the computer all the time."

"So are you like that? Do you have no friends and just sit at the computer all the time?"

"No. But what if this means I'm going to turn *into* a nerd?"

"I don't think that's how it works," I say. "I don't think you go from having friends to having no friends just because you got glasses."

"You just want to believe that because you wear glasses." Damn, I say to myself. I've gotta try contacts again.

"Here's what I don't get," I say, deciding not to try to deprogram her all at once. "How come you couldn't tell your mom this was happening? Maybe she could help. Maybe you could get contacts or something."

"Oh, no. You don't know my mom. She'll say I'm too young. And she'll say it's what's on your *inside* that counts . . . not your outside."

"Do you think that's true? It's what's on your inside that counts?"

"Yes, I think it's true. But my mom . . ." She hesitates for a long time. She doesn't want to think her mom is wrong about anything. "She doesn't get it. She thinks everybody can just look however they want, but she doesn't have to see Lisa every day."

So the only thing Marty can think to do, although she's not really thinking consciously in the sense of rational planning, is to get sick and stay home from school. Easy problem, right? If only all of child therapy were so easy. With most kids who demonstrate school avoidance, the problem is a lot more obscure. This one seems refreshingly straightforward. And the solution is . . . Uh-oh. What is the solution? As I think about how to talk to Marty's mom and dad, suddenly I understand more clearly why her solution seemed to her to be the best one.

At this point, readers who have been around the block a few times might be wondering, "What's the big deal? Kids have always tormented other kids for wearing glasses." That is indeed the case, but this particular form of torment is something new and much more virulent than good old-fashioned name-calling. Name-calling among younger kids is always relatively straightforward and unitary: Younger kids sometimes make fun of someone who seems to be different or strange because of the one thing that makes them seem different or strange. Younger kids who are different than their peers might be mocked for wearing glasses, walking with a limp, or talking with an accent, because that one thing makes them unusual. But, in younger kids, the thing that is mocked is only one thing, it is not a signifier of a complex devalued identity. For Marty, wearing glasses isn't just about wearing glasses; it's also about *being* or, worse yet, *becoming* something she doesn't understand. And how could she? She doesn't watch a lot of television. She doesn't get the whole complex relationship of computers to *Star Trek* and deodorant and SAT scores and sex and Dungeons & Dragons and *Beauty and the Geek*. And how could she understand all that? It takes a lot of weird cultural indoctrination to get all that, and she's still uninitiated. In fact, this very nasty episode is the first time she's ever really thought about nerds or geeks at all.

This is what makes Marty's experience different from the experience of countless generations of kids who got picked on when they first got their glasses. Marty is experiencing a category system, the nerd/geek identity, borrowed from adolescence and developed in the cognitive world of adolescence. But it is being imposed on a fourth-grader who thinks like a fourth-grader, and fourth-graders don't get a lot of stuff that adolescents get. It is, in fact, the bracket creep that goes along with the tween experience that makes Marty, and so many kids like her, miserable.

We will have much more to say about tweens, but let's just start with the obvious. The tween experience is, first and foremost, a marketing phenomenon. Along about the early 1990s, marketers figured out something that parents had known all along: Younger siblings are in a hurry to act like teenagers. Nine- and ten-year-olds have always wanted to emulate their older brothers and sisters, and parents have always responded with a firm "Not yet." Teenagerdom has always been demarcated fairly cleanly, because the bodily changes of adolescence are relatively clear. Although the timing of adolescent changes is variable, parents in the relatively recent past could usually know when to treat their child like a teenager just by looking at him or her: When the child had acne or began to need a shave or a bra, it was time for the rules to change.

But that was in the simple old days before we had tweens. The enormous power of the market forces unleashed by the tween phenomenon is hard to describe, but here are a few indicators: It is estimated that children aged eight to thirteen control $335 billion in family purchasing power. Marketers of new products, including television shows, hair products, and teenage girl singers, regularly consult the GIA—the Girls' Intelligence Agency—which uses a network of tween girls' slumber parties to gather information on what girls want as well as to affect girls' purchasing decisions through the strategic use of tween "alpha girls," who are paid to get a company's message or product out to the target audience. Whether one is trying to sell cell phones, fashion accessories, or records, the vast power of eight- to thirteen-year-olds hungering to be thirteen- to eighteen-year-olds is a wave that has engulfed all contemporary kids and their unfortunate parents. Although the marketing push has focused largely on girls, the new push to capture the less developed tween boy market is cited as the next big thing in marketing to kids.

The result of all this marketing push is the powerful indoctrination into adolescent culture of all sorts of children who are not, cognitively and emotionally speaking, adolescents. Indeed, one of the biggest problems of the nerd/geek stereotype is that it is, through the unavoidable trickling down of adolescent culture, embraced by kids who think like kids. This is why so many parents fail to see the dark side of nerd/geek stereotyping: They think it is something invented by and applied to high school kids. And high school kids are a lot more savvy about their identities; they know they can change their spots. Kids in high school do it all the time. Simply by changing their clothes and their hair and their taste in music, they can change their peers and (not immediately but in fairly short order) thus change the way they are thought of by other kids. The fluidity of identity that is a hallmark of adolescence goes along with the cognitive maturity afforded by real biological adolescence: Kids with more adultlike brains see social categories as relative and socially created, and see themselves as participants in the act of creation of themselves and thus of the social orders of high school.

But middle school kids and late-elementary-school kids—tweens—don't think like that. As a result, they eagerly seek information about the social categories of high school so that they *know what they already are.* This is why there is a market for "Are you a nerd?" self-tests. The question is powerful only for the kids who don't know the answer but think there *is* an answer and feel desperate to find it: kids in fourth through eighth grade. These are precisely the kids who should be protected from nerd/geek stereotypes, because, as we have seen, they use these rigid stereotypes to make decisions (like concluding that "taking advanced math and science is for nerds") that affect their school careers for several years.

IDENTITY, YOUTH, AND SHOPPING

In order to see how much identity formation has changed, we need to go back several decades in the history of American psychology. Erik Erikson, the psychoanalyst who coined the term "identity crisis," published his pioneering work *Childhood and Society* in 1950. In this groundbreaking book, Erikson went beyond psychoanalytic orthodoxy, which had until then emphasized worldwide universals in psychological development, to describe the unique relationships among psychological development, family pressures, and cultural change. The Danish-born Erikson was fascinated by American youth, and he described in loving detail what it meant to be an American kid. He marveled at the openness of American society, and, for all we might snicker at the idea of the cultural "openness" of America in the 1950s, he described a society that was the most flexible in the world: There was nowhere else where kids were allowed to imagine and enact such an unfixed set of social roles.

Erikson described, in several of his works, the task of adolescence as identity formation. Identity formation, for Erikson, was a piece of psychological work that came along with puberty: Imagining oneself as a sexual adult meant opening the door to imagining oneself as an adult in all sorts of ways. Teenagers had to figure out, then, who they were sexually, occupationally, and socially all at once and all in a relatively brief space of time. This psychological work was accompanied by a great deal of experimentation, uncertainty, and a sense of psychological crisis. Kids knew, then, that they needed to make some big decisions, decisions that would not be made for them, as they were in most other parts of the world. In a time when many kids did not go to college, the occupational part needed to be settled by the time high school was over, so the whole process was necessarily compact, and much of the urgency Erikson described was associated with the pressure of time nipping at teenaged heels. After all, Erikson's next stage of human development, that of developing intimacy, began roughly when people were in their early twenties and thinking about settling down to raise a family. (This was in an era when people married, on average, at age twenty-two, much younger than the current median age of 26.7 for men and 25.1 for women.) Certainly the stage of figuring out who you were, personally and occupationally, had to be done in time to support the family and start transmitting internalized values to the next generation.

Until puberty, for Erikson, people were essentially children. We might marvel at this, but we can remember that Erikson was not making things up out of whole cloth or making pronouncements based on some theoretical imperative; he was basing his descriptions of developmental stages on what he saw around him in his practice and in his world. Kids were kids until they hit puberty, and they did the things kids did: The boys played ball and collected rocks and baseball cards, and the girls dressed up and played with dolls and babysat; if they were very lucky, they rode horses, and if not they read about riding horses. The nostalgic idea of the "innocence" of the 1950s is absurd when applied to teenagers; the innocence of prewar America was shattered by World War II, and teenagers in the 1950s were certainly sexual, and sexually active, beings. But one might say truthfully that children, meaning people who had not yet reached puberty, were innocent in the 1950s and even the 1960s and 1970s, because the rampant sexualization of kids by popular culture had not yet occurred.

What would Erikson have made of the following?

It's hard to write this without sounding like a prig. But it's just as hard to erase the images that planted the idea for this essay, so here goes. The scene is a middle school auditorium, where girls in teams of three or four are bopping to pop songs at a student talent show. Not bopping, actually, but doing elaborately choreographed re-creations of music videos, in tiny skirts or tight shorts, with bare bellies, rouged cheeks and glittery eyes.

They writhe and strut, shake their bottoms, splay their legs, thrust their chests out and in and out again. Some straddle empty chairs, like lap dancers without laps. They don't smile much. Their faces are locked from grim exertion, from all that leaping up and lying down without poles to hold on to. "Don't stop, don't stop," sings Janet Jackson, all whispery. "Jerk it like you're making it choke . . . Ohh. I'm so stimulated. Feel so X-rated." The girls spend a lot of time lying on the floor. They are in the sixth, seventh and eighth grades.

As each routine ends, parents and siblings cheer, whistle and applaud. I just sit there, not fully comprehending. It's my first suburban Long Island middle school talent show. I'm with my daughter, who is ten and hadn't warned me. I'm not sure what I had expected, but it wasn't this. It was something different. Something younger. Something that didn't make the girls look so . . . one-dimensional.

This account, from "Middle School Girls Gone Wild" by Lawrence Downes, appeared in *The New York Times* in late 2006. The father is obviously distressed, as are so many other parents of his generation, because of what he rightly sees as something grotesque: the trickling down of adolescent culture, and adolescent concerns, into a group of kids who are not biologically or cognitively ready for those concerns. This is the

sense of disgust that accompanied much of America's response to the videos of little JonBenét Ramsey before her
tragic murder: "That girl can't possibly know what she's doing,
so why is she acting like that?" The girls in this talent show were
ten, not four, but the response is the same: There is something
unnatural in seeing people who are not sexually mature acting
like they are. Most parents know instinctively that this is dangerous, especially for girls, but they don't know how to stop it.

It is obvious in such a culture that Erikson's theory no
longer applies. The linking of the developmental task of identity formation with sexual maturity has obviously come apart in
a large segment of contemporary kids, and psychological theory has to change to conform to new realities. Gil Noam, a
developmental and clinical psychologist at Harvard Medical
School, attempts to fill this gap by positing a new stage in
development that precedes the old Eriksonian stage of "identity versus role confusion." Noam takes note of the high standard of individual development required for true identity
consolidation and points out that most early adolescents do
not have the ego strength to reach this level of individual self-
knowledge; indeed, many people never reach, in their whole
lifetime, the level of identity integration that Erikson describes
as the end of normal adolescence. Noam posits a new stage of
psychological development that he calls the mutual-inclusive
or "belonging-versus-rejection" stage. Noam describes some
of the issues that characterize normal development in this
stage:

- Self strongly defined by group
- Self defined through others' eyes

- Sense of belonging essential to well-being
- Hypervigilance about being liked and accepted

Noam locates the ages for this new stage from approximately eleven to thirteen years of age, what we used to call "early adolescence." What Noam fails to offer in his account is a discussion of the pseudomaturity involved when this stage is pushed downward by the effects of media culture. What tween marketers discovered in the 1990s was that a stage of intense anxiety about "belonging" is a marketers' dream. The combination of young teenagers who are terribly anxious about being left out and parents of smaller families with more disposable income to help kids not feel left out has been a combustible mix, from a marketing point of view. And the cognitive changes of adolescence, which make all this meaningful psychologically for kids who really are eleven to thirteen, are absent for kids who are eight to eleven. Tweens get the huge marketing push, but they still think like kids, which means rigidity, black-and-white thinking, and plain old confusion about how to behave. Younger kids trying to be older are trying to fit in with social groups, tribes, or identities that do not, and should not, make sense to them, because these identities are based on sexual urgencies that are simply not present. So what we get are girls who, in the not-too-distant past, were riding horses and playing with dolls now pole-dancing in the middle school talent show. And we get, increasingly, boys who were once collecting baseball cards now trying to figure out how to act like studs (whatever that means to preadolescent boys). The development might be called pseudo-self-consciousness, the precocious attention to and preoccupation with sexual display that used to be the province of adolescence now moving down into childhood.

THE NERD IDENTITY
AS SAFE HARBOR

Where do nerds fit into all this? It is not, after all, girl nerds who are shaking their booties at the Long Island middle school talent show. It is precisely not nerds who are doing that. Nerds wouldn't be caught dead doing something like that; they wouldn't know how, and they wouldn't be interested. Nerd-labeled kids are, in fact, curiously immune from the rampant sexualization and, more generally, adultization of preteen culture. Here we might notice one of the very best things about nerds, or at least nerd-labeled kids: They act like children, and, when they actually are children, it's really very refreshing.

It is precisely the lack of self-consciousness that sets nerdy kids apart from non-nerdy kids. In saying this, I am referring to the pseudo-self-consciousness imposed by the tweeny culture; the shame imparted to kids who do not yet feel ready to act like grown-ups but still act like kids. Nerdy kids are self-conscious enough, God knows, when it comes to high school, when they are tortured by the more or less "real" self-consciousness that goes with movement into the early stages of cognitive adulthood. The natural shyness of some kids labeled as nerdy is magnified a hundredfold by the normal self-consciousness of adolescence, and then these kids do really retreat to the safety of their computer terminals. But there is that earlier sense of unself-consciousness, that almost opaque immunity to shaming, that makes nerdy kids endearing to adults: They are still, somehow, clueless about how they appear and therefore still tractable, because they are not aware of how they seem to their peers.

Let's take another example from the distant past. Well, not distant in my case, but it certainly seems distant in the early twenty-first century. When I was a kid, there was an almost universal participation in what is now seen as a very nerdy activity: scouting. Throughout most of elementary school, every boy in my class was a Cub Scout. Den meetings (for those not in the know, the "den" was the little local group of Cub Scouts, the smallest unit of organization in Scout Nation) were held after school at the home of a kid who lived a couple of blocks from school, and we were supposed to attend wearing our Cub Scout uniforms. That meant that every Scout— that is, every boy in the class—proudly wore his Cub Scout uniform to school on the days of den meetings because there was no time to go home and change, and, besides, it made one feel proud and masculine to wear the uniform to school. Around the end of elementary school—that is, around age eleven or twelve—there was the transition to Boy Scouts, and all the bigness that went along with it: sleepaway camps and jamborees and much more adultlike responsibility. A lot of kids I knew dropped out of scouting then, because they had other activities going on: They had started to branch out into music lessons and more serious sports, and no longer had time for scouting. But a lot of kids stayed in, and they continued to wear their uniforms on occasion to junior high school, with nary a whisper or snicker behind the back. It was simply one among a lot of other things that kids did, and kids in junior high school were still proud of their merit badges and eager to show them off to their non-Scout friends and even their girlfriends.

Fast-forward to the present day. Can you imagine such a thing? In my work as a child therapist, I occasionally look to make a referral to a Cub Scout or Boy Scout troop for a particular kind of kid: a kid who is eager and kind but who has been getting kicked around a little too much by his peers—the kind of kid who can really enjoy and benefit from the peer interaction in the context of adult supervision that is still the sine qua non of scouting. But I can't find a Scout troop to refer anyone to. They seem to have disappeared, or gone way underground like the early Christians. They are nowhere, apparently, where I am. And if they do exist, they sure don't wear their uniforms to school. Scouts are routinely ridiculed as nerds and geeks, much to the disappointment of generations of Scout leaders who credit the Boy Scouts of America for so much character education. A typical response among contemporary kids is the one found in the readers' forum of the *Detroit Free Press* after the death of Gerald Ford. Ford, who had been an Eagle Scout and a scoutmaster, was eulogized in print for his uprightness, as exemplified by his participation in scouting. But one reader needed to set the record straight, as he did in his comment in the newspaper's online forum: "Hey scoutdad, let me clue you in. Boy scouts are NERDS. They get picked on in school. An Eagle Scout is a grown up nerd that has no friends. You are definitaly [sic] an eagle scout. Nerd." Thanks for that clarification, kid. God forbid we should let Boy Scouts get away with thinking they are doing something interesting or prosocial or admirable.

Scouts are so nerdy they need to be ostracized, even if they are former presidents of the United States. Kids who are now involved in old-fashioned childish activities are routinely vilified, even by adults. Indeed, one of the things that is really new and gives nerd/geek stereotypes their special twenty-first-century meanness is adult participation in what used to be child-to-child cruelty. Desperate adults trying to prove they are still young bash unhip kids to show how hip they are to the ways of the young. So we have Joel Stein, for example, writing in the *Los Angeles Times* in February 2007 about the reintroduction of dollar coins by the U.S. Treasury, going out of his way to bash coin collectors: "[The new dollar coins] feature a different president, in order, at four a year, much like the state quarters that have gripped the nation's socially awkward eight-year-old boys." Okay, Joel. So we know you know kids look down on coin collecting; even among eight-year-old boys only the "socially awkward" would even think of participating. But just out of curiosity, what would you have those boys do instead, since coin collecting is so hopelessly unhip? Play in a garage band? Try to feel up their eight-year-old girlfriends? What? We appreciate how important it is to vilify un-hip kids, but let's go all the way and specify the rules so kids will know exactly what they're supposed to do.

This kind of thing might seem like an easy answer for parents of nerd-labeled kids: All we need to do is instruct them in what not to do, like join the Boy Scouts or collect coins. All we need to do is pay attention and read the papers so we know who trendsetters like Joel Stein feel contempt for and then get our nerd-labeled kids to shape up. End of story, right? The unhip get wise, and everyone is happier.

Except that is not what the parents of nerd-labeled kids tend to do. As nine-year-old Marty told me when she was getting her glasses, she knows what her mother will say: "It doesn't matter how you look." "What matters is what's inside." "Who cares what other kids think?" "Beauty's only skin deep." Marty's mother, who is less than fashionable, thinks people who are fashionable are a little shallow, and she wants to impart these values to her kid. So she doesn't really take it too seriously when Marty is brutally savaged every day by her ex-friend Lisa. But then, as Marty says, "Mom doesn't have to go to school with her."

The question of parenting values is important here for several reasons. Since this is an age when brain biology and genetics are the sexiest thing going in psychology, people like doctors and scientists tend to forget cultural transmission as a useful explanatory factor, in this case a factor that might explain why nerd-labeled or geeky kids sometimes seem to have equally nerd-labelable or geekoid parents. It might be that Asperger's syndrome, or some mild version thereof, is heritable (see chapter 4). But what is more likely is that parents tend to transmit their values to their kids, and parents who are antifashion, anti-surface, or antiappearance, for whatever reason, might also feel that it is not important how their kids look to their peers.

Take the example of Andy, a thirteen-year-old seventh-grader whose mother consulted with me informally about his social difficulties. Andy was a very sophisticated techie kid who was already programming independently, inventing games and applications for his own use. He was also being mercilessly teased in school for being nerdy and geeky because he was still wearing sweatpants to school, a crime of no small proportion in seventh grade. Sweatpants in school are for little kids, and Andy, who was wearing them for comfort, was terribly embarrassed about how he was being teased. There was an obvious solution, but of course it was less than obvious to Andy's mother.

"What do all the other kids wear to school?" I asked.

"Well, jeans, I guess. Yes. Andy says they all wear jeans."

"So why not get him some jeans to wear to school?"

"Well . . . he's comfortable in sweatpants."

"True. But he gets teased all the time. So, since he says he doesn't want to be teased, why not get him the jeans and dump the sweatpants?"

"Don't you think that would be sending the wrong message?"

Sometimes it's best to play dumb. "Wrong message? What's the message?"

"That appearance is important. Do we want to teach Andy that if kids make fun of your appearance, you should change it . . . *just to fit in?*"

God forbid he should fit in, I think. But looking at his mother, in her busted-out clogs and ill-fitting corduroy slacks and elderly college sweatshirt, it occurs to me that fitting into the moderately fashionable urban setting where we are meeting is not really one of her priorities. More to the point, I realize that when I saw her husband earlier in the day, he was wearing sweatpants, and it wasn't at the gym. These people, academics but not technology workers, seem to have absolutely no interest in their appearance.

"Well, here's the deal," I say. "He's in seventh grade, the cruelest grade known to humankind. I think he probably has good values already by now, and he's not a superficial kid. A little attention to his appearance—if that's what he wants for himself—may not be so bad." In other words, he's not you. Or to paraphrase my child patient Marty, "You don't have to be in seventh grade, and he does."

But Andy's mother is shocked by this suggestion. It has never occurred to her, literally never, to buy him some jeans to wear to school so he won't be teased. It's like I'm suggesting a heinous crime. She can't wrap her mind around the concept. She has defined herself as well as her family as antimaterialistic, and so going along to get along is equivalent to being a pervert. A lot of nerd-labeled kids have parents who fall on this continuum: They are deeply religious, or deeply anticapitalist, or somehow just deeply opposed to the hegemonic order of seventh grade, and their kids know this and often despair of it, because they are afraid even to suggest doing something that will free them from the nerd label.

When I saw Andy's father months later, he reported that Andy was a new man. He was wearing jeans to school, and the kids stopped teasing him overnight. He felt better about himself and better about school than he had in years. He thanked me profusely for my brilliant suggestion. "Oh, shucks," I said, digging the toe of my shoe into the dirt at my feet. "It's all in a day's work." These parents, unlike many others, were flexible enough to see the obvious when it was pointed out to them,

and after they got over the initial shock, they were embarrassed about how they had contributed to their son's misery.

Luckily, in Andy's case, the treatment worked. In the case of
many other kids, this treatment does not. And why should it?
Parents who are struggling against the tide of crap washing over
their kids should be applauded for giving it the old college try.
Those who support their kids in scouting or going to religious
school or those who prevent them from watching television or
turn off the instant-messaging software so they actually do their
homework are fighting a heroic battle. The hegemonic order of
seventh grade, which often features a social hierarchy based on
clothes, hair products, and whose cell phone has the coolest features, is worthy of being resisted.

But the seventh-grade hegemon cannot be resisted forever,
and it cannot be resisted categorically. Blue jeans may not be the
place to draw the line. Trying to find the balance between a family's occasionally countercultural values and a middle school
kid's need to fit in can be exhausting. It is this exhaustion that
causes many families with idiosyncratic values, whether these
values are religious or political or intellectual, to choose the
home-schooling route: If there are no peers (except other home-
schooled kids), there are no peers to mock you because your
brand-new expensive cell phone still doesn't have enough features. But many parents of nerd-labeled kids don't home-school
and don't feel the need to. These are parents who don't see how
tough it is for their kids because they don't feel social pressure
so acutely. They have successfully resisted conformity for so
long that they have forgotten how hard it is to do. They don't
know that buying the blue jeans or the contact lenses may not
be the same thing as selling your child down the river.

NERD ENVY

We cannot leave this topic without bringing up the possibility that is obvious to a psychodynamic psychologist but may seem absurd to most others. This possibility is that one reason nerds and geeks are vilified, at least in middle school, is because other kids envy them. When you look at the vituperation nerd-labeled kids are subjected to, it's hard to imagine them as enviable. But maybe the envy comes first, and maybe the envy is largely unconscious. Maybe a lot of kids would secretly like to be nerdy. How might that be?

Psychoanalytic theorists have long posited that developmental stages or phases involve children in a sense of loss. This is most clear, and intuitively obvious, in toddlerhood and early childhood, when being a "big boy" or a "big girl," as much as it is valued by kids, means losing a cherished piece of babyhood. Giving up the pacifier, giving up the bottle and switching to a cup, giving up the crib or the parental bed for the "big-boy bed," are all important milestones, but the reason parents have to talk them up so much is that there is a normal sense of regret attendant on leaving the comforts of babyhood behind.

There is no reason to suppose that this sense of regret does not continue. After early childhood is over, this is only clear at times of developmental crisis. One can certainly see it in the craziness of so many high school seniors who are desperately looking forward to college while, at the same time, they are terribly sad and anxious about leaving their friends and the comforts of home. Growing up always involves loss and regret, and for children it also involves anger at those who still get to have what they are losing. The anger and contempt kids express toward "babies" or kids who are babyish is motivated, in large part, by this kind of envy: How come you still get to have a bottle, when I have to give it up? How come you still get to sleep with Mom and Dad?

So it seems possible, then, that some of the contempt nerd-labeling kids direct toward the nerd-labeled is of this same form. How come you still feel so confident? How come you aren't frantic about your hair? How come you can wear sweatpants because they feel comfortable, when I have to feel ugly no matter what I wear? How come you can still get excited about getting the answers right, when I'm supposed to feel excited about getting answers wrong? How is that you think the tape on your glasses is invisible? This is structurally very much like the kid version of the often expressed envy that people who have lost their religious faith express toward people who still have it: How come you still get to feel so safe when I have to feel so unsafe?

The awful truth is that nerd-labeled kids will get wise soon enough. They may just be a little slower to wise up to the incredible pressure to be superficial that all kids now face. But when they do wise up, it will be just as awful for them as it is for kids who tween up early, or worse. Nobody gets out unscathed. Punishing middle school kids who are still relatively unself-conscious is an unattractive pursuit, especially for grown-ups who should know better, and trying to protect them by ignoring the fierceness of the world they live in doesn't help too much, either. As usual, it's up to us to find the middle ground and hold on to it the best we can. But we can, in passing, note that we might have some regrets of our own when we think hateful thoughts about nerdy kids. We might remember the days when we proudly wore our Boy Scout—or Girl Scout—uniforms to school and were excited to feel the impressive weight of merit badges on our chests.

8.

I'M NOT BORING
YOU, AM I?

· OR ·

WHAT IS THIS THING CALLED
THE SILMARILLION?

A ndy is thirteen. He prides himself on being "inter-
tribal": He says he gets along with everybody in his
middle school. He plays soccer, and he reads a lot, and,
although he doesn't think of himself as "preppy," he gets along
with all the "preppy" kids. "I even have friends who are nerds,"
he says, sort of proudly, as if he were Leonard Bernstein invit-
ing the Black Panthers to dinner. "Oh?" I say. "Are there nerds
in your school?"

So we're off and running. He lists the characteristic characteristics, the pocket protectors, the glasses, the too-short
pants, and the white socks. And the things they do for fun.
"Like what?" "Warhammer," he says emphatically. "They all
play Warhammer, all the time." Later, when I ask him which of
all those things—the glasses, the pants, all of it (he admits
that he has never seen a kid in his school wearing a pocket

protector)—is the one thing that really makes a kid nerdy? I read back the list. What's the ultimate badge of nerdiness?

"Warhammer." He says emphatically.

Meanwhile, in the Dark Elf kingdom of Naggaroth, the Seers of Ghrond continue their unceasing study of the distant Chaos Maelstrom. Suddenly, there is a marked shift in the nebulous swirls of color and shape. The Seers watch intently, studying the ominous new patterns. When they are confident of their readings, the Seers dispatch a messenger south to Naggarond aboard a swift Black Pegasus. Great events are about to unfold in the world, and the Witch King must be informed.

Days later, Malekith, Lord of the Dark Elves, reads the dispatch from Ghrond. The Chaos god Tzeentch has found himself a new Champion. The followers of the Changer of Ways have assembled a great warhost for his herald and are preparing to launch a massive incursion into the lands of men, the Empire his likely target.

Malekith ponders the message. . . . If the forces of Chaos launch an attack while the Empire is weakened by the plague, the Emperor will have no choice but to call upon the nearby Dwarfs for reinforcement. With the aid of the Dwarfs, it is possible the Chaos host might be turned back. If, however, the folk of the mountains are unable to come to the Empire's defense, Emperor Karl Franz will be forced to turn to the High Elves of Ulthuan. Malekith is doubtful that his kinsmen will abandon the great nation of men in its hour of need, for doing so might deprive the High Elves of a valuable ally. No . . . the High Elves will respond, and will likely send several legions of warriors to repulse the Chaos attack, leaving Ulthuan vulnerable.

When the Chaos moon eclipses the light of the sun, the dispatch concludes, the forces of Chaos will begin their march southward. Time is short, and there is much to do.

Time is indeed short, and there is always much to do. Especially when you play Warhammer, which involves the assembly and painting of lots and lots of little figures that you use to play the tabletop version of the game. Warhammer was first introduced in 1983 as a tabletop game in which the moves are controlled with standard dice. As a tabletop game, it has a long and distinguished provenance: It is sort of like a very detailed version of Risk, the Parker Brothers "game of global domination" reported to have been a favorite of President George W. Bush when he was in college. In Risk, players have territories, and they move against each other on a game board with a map of the real world. But the game pieces are all the same, and the map of the world that is being symbolically dominated is a familiar map: the known world.

In Warhammer, the figures are painted and decorated by the players themselves, so in one way it is like what making model airplanes or ships used to be for kids who did that kind of thing. The pieces are painstakingly painted, and there are competitions in which Warhammer players are awarded prizes for their creative and/or detailed Warhammer-figure painting. There is also a detailed map of a fantasy world, the realm of Azeroth (for the tabletop game), and a very detailed story that goes along with each version of the game. The stories are like the passage quoted above, which is actually a bit of backstory from the online computer version of Warhammer, called Warhammer Part II: Dark Omens. These stories, too, have their provenance: Take equal parts *The Lord of the Rings* and *Conan the Barbarian*, add several milligrams of some steroidal power-enhancing formula, put them in a word blender, blend on high for two minutes, and presto! You have yet another story for Warhammer, replete with men, elves, dwarves, goblins, and ogres and demons of various kinds. There is a lot of brute strength and a lot of magic, and the often scantily clad women are no shrinking violets.

Warhammer exists at a crossroad, so to speak, and it is the particular crossroad that leads right through middle school. It appeals to kids and adults who love strategy games as well as kids and adults who love mastering a huge amount of detailed knowledge. Games like this have been around for a long time. In the 1950s and 1960s, Avalon Hill published games based on battles in the Civil War or World War II that required sophisticated strategy, detailed maps of battlefields, and crafty deployment of resources—games like Gettysburg and Anzio—that teenagers and adults played for hours or days. Warhammer is like those games, but it adds the modeling component, a sure-fire hit with many late-elementary-school and middle school kids and the late-elementary kid in all of us.

It also incorporates the vocabulary, so to speak, of the godfather of all role-playing games, Dungeons & Dragons. D&D, first published in 1974 and still the most popular role-playing game, is credited with inventing the role-playing–game (RPG) category. D&D has, as its own spiritual ancestor, most kids' fascination with medieval times and Celtic mythology, including the tales of King Arthur or the novels of Sir Walter Scott.

Indeed, in another time, the kids who are now so enthusiastically playing Warhammer might have been reading *Ivanhoe*. It also is a direct descendant of Tolkien and Conan, along with many other pulp-fiction sources. RPGs have now become a huge industry in their own right, with the establishment of MMORPGs, or massively multiplayer online role-playing games, like the online version of Warhammer or the even more massively popular World of Warcraft. In these games, players select their own avatars, which have life stories and specific skills, reputations, and tools, and compete against the environment or against each other as they annihilate other characters at will. In particular, World of Warcraft, which has an alternative economic system in which real grown-ups pay lots of real money to acquire other players' characters or skills, is a far cry from the more innocent world of tabletop Warhammer, despite the surface similarities.

NERDS AND FANTASY: JUST THE FACTS

So when a kid like Andy, and all the other Andys of the middle school world, identify Warhammer as the ultimate in nerdity, what exactly are they saying? The brief description given above is almost too brief to do it justice: Warhammer encompasses a whole world of detail. But if we identify the essential components of Warhammer, we might go some way toward understanding what it is about Warhammer and games like it that proclaim its devotees as nerds.

To separate the elements that make up the appeal of

Warhammer, we might start with the following: (a) it is strategic; (b) it requires making or painting little figures or models; (c) it is an incredibly detailed world; and (d) it is about unhuman beings—elves and trolls and wizards and the like—as well as human beings. It cannot be the fact that it is played on a computer, because the tabletop version of Warhammer does not require a computer. And games played on a computer, if we include all the games available using the Sony PlayStation or Xbox or Wii game machines, are a huge entertainment category. But boys, and men, who play Grand Theft Auto are not called nerds or geeks. Indeed, if every teenage or college kid who played games at a computer or video terminal were called a nerd, there would be no one left to do the name-calling. There must be something else about certain kinds of fantasy games that set off the alarms for the nerd police.

Is it the strategy aspect of Warhammer? As we noted, almost all games played by kids and adults include some element of strategy, except the card games that little kids play that are prestrategic and based on chance, like War, or based on simple matching, like Go Fish. Board games with searching and hiding strategies, like Stratego or Battleship, are not bastions of nerdity; kids play them and enjoy them without adding a whole lot of surplus cultural meaning. Even chess, the game traditionally associated with genius, is not necessarily vilified by schoolkids, because they can master the rules fairly quickly: kids who are not geniuses can play chess and enjoy it at a low level of play, and many kids do just that. People who play Risk, whether kids or adults, are not usually called Risk nerds. The use of strategy as an element of all games seems to preclude the strategy aspect itself as the dead giveaway of nerdity.

The little figures or models don't seem especially promising, either. Although building and painting models is in decline among kids, there are other similar activities that have taken their place: building massively complex Lego ships, rockets, and planes, for example. Building and painting little tiny figures—doing it—requires a passion for precision (see chapter 6), which, while not mathematical or scientific, does mean patience and the ability to delay gratification. Not every kid can do that. But, once again, these "anal" activities seem to be off the nerd-labelers' radar screens. There is no nerd self-test I have yet encountered that asks questions about participation in building or making models; it's just not part of the stereotype, probably because of its long provenance and association with stereotypical masculinity. And building and making models is close enough to tinkering itself, the ennobled activity of American Men of Action, that it is safe from association with the nerd/geek stereotype. Every American man has his workshop, the tinkerer's Valhalla, and in that Valhalla a passion for precision is allowed to flourish without suffering the withering contempt of one's fellows. No, it's not making the little figures that makes Warhammer the sine qua non of nerdity.

In addition to being a strategy game and requiring the little figures (absent in the online version played by older people), Warhammer shares another feature with older strategy games: It is an incredibly detailed world. A look at the manual or the map or the website for Warhammer makes it immediately clear that mastering a great deal of backstory will be required. It's like coming into a soap opera in the middle of a particularly lurid and complicated story arc: It's very difficult to figure out, on one viewing, just *why* Angie's yen for T.J. is so illicit, so shocking, or so forbidden. Soap opera magazines or online plot summaries are only too happy to oblige by providing the backstory, but it does require a certain amount of motivation even to master this relatively familiar world. But since these stories take place in Everytown, USA, or some equivalent (Pine Valley, etc.), it's not that difficult. It's probably either just plain old lust or greed in equal measures that drives these people to do the dramatic things they sometimes do.

But the world of Warhammer is different. The backstory itself, which is presumably there to help people get oriented, is not for the faint of heart. You can tell by all the "however" and "meanwhile." Let's look at it again:

> If, however, the folk of the mountains are unable to come to the Empire's defense, Emperor Karl Franz will be forced to turn to the High Elves of Ulthuan. Malekith is doubtful that his kinsmen will abandon the great nation of men in its hour of need, for doing so might deprive the High Elves of a valuable ally. No . . . the High Elves will respond, and will likely send several legions of warriors to repulse the Chaos attack, leaving Ulthuan vulnerable.

Does this draw you in? Does it make you curious about who, exactly, these beings are, and how they know so much about each other ("No . . . the High Elves will respond . . ."), while you know nothing about them at all? For many people, this kind of text induces despair: There is too much to master all at once, and, since it's supposed to be fun, why bother? It chases people away; it's overwhelming.

But if it draws you in, who are you? Whoever you are, you probably share one thing with most players of RPGs, online, tabletop, or live action: You are a person with a lot of time on your hands. We can borrow the economic notion of entry cost here to describe what's going on: All of these fantasy worlds have a very high entry cost. It takes the investment of a lot of time to get far enough into the action to start having fun. And the notion of entry cost is one thing that separates the nerd-labeled from the nerd-labelers: Some people just can't stand the delay and the amount of effort that such a project requires. It takes too long, and it's experienced as boring or too hard or too much like schoolwork. Kids who hate this kind of thing aren't lazy; they will spend half their lives practicing their layups or doing soccer drills or practicing their guitar licks. But the idea of voluntarily taking on a tremendous amount of new complicated information in the form of fantasy backstories or game instructions is just too much work.

One can see the entry-cost effect in nerd self-tests and in the behavior of nerd-labelers most visibly when the entry cost changes. Take *The Lord of the Rings*, for example. When the only way to experience *The Lord of the Rings* was by reading it, a lot of kids did not. The length of the trilogy, its heft, is daunting enough, and then there are all those names to remember. The Hobbits, who have names like Frodo and Sam, are okay, but once you get to Rivendell and the books start sprouting Elvish names like exotic weeds—Lúthien Tenúviel and Arwen Undómiel, not to mention all those names that are so similar, like Elrond, Elladan, Elrohir, etc.—many kids as well as their elders gave up. And *The Lord of the Rings* was a staple on nerd self-tests: If you had read it, you were by definition a nerd or geek. But now that it has been made into a lush, easy-to-watch, thrilling movie, it is no longer a nerd shibboleth. The effort has been drained out of it. What is left in the movie is a thrilling, action-packed adventure story with beautiful movie stars cavorting around in great costumes and lots and lots of horses. What is gone are the runes and the weird names and the daunting recounting of origin myths, like how the Elves came to Middle-earth, and endless recitation of lineages that make the Old Testament seem like a comic book by comparison. Now that it is accessible, lots of people know it and love it, and it is no longer nerdy or geeky to know who Gandalf is or to refer to an enemy as being like Sauron or Gollum.

In the pre–Liv-Tyler-as-Arwen-Undómiel days, what was nerdy about *The Lord of the Rings* was the effort it took to enjoy it. Now the only way it remains a nerd shibboleth is if you have read the real backstory: *The Silmarillion*, J. R. R. Tolkien's posthumous book about the prehistory of the Elves and the origins of their ancient curses and powers. *The Silmarillion* is really hard to read, because it is not terribly dramatic: The battles and curses are recounted but not described, so it is hard to picture, and the names are beyond confusing. The only people who read it are people who have already read *The Lord of the Rings* and just want more and who have an extraordinarily high threshold for tedium. But maybe someday it too will be made into a movie, and then those few people who know the difference between Melkor and Morgoth will be rescued from terminal geekiness.

THE WHOLE WIZARD THING

Then there's the whole wizard thing itself. As we have seen, Warhammer reeks of nerdity not because it a strategy experience and not because of painting all the little figurines. The effortful backstory is a major factor in the nerdity of Warhammer, but the backstory is about something particular. There is something more to it than complication, and that something is the nature of magic and wizardry as the content of the complicated backstory. As we saw in chapter 6, there are many areas of noncompulsory human activity that have a high entry cost—once again, fly-fishing comes to mind—and do not carry the nerd/geek label. But immersion in complex high-entry-cost activities that involve certain kinds of fantasy and magic is not fly-fishing. There is something else about magic and wizardry that puts off nerd-labeling kids, certainly by the time they get to middle school.

That thing about magic and its association with nerdity is the simple fact that magic is disreputable because magic undoes natural advantages. Magic is an equalizer, in the very same sense that guns in the Old West were described as "equalizers." What guns equalized, of course, was physical prowess: Physical strength, as the ultimate resource to be used in asserting power and winning conflicts, was no longer the great asset it had once been. Big men could be brought down by little men if the little men had guns. Countless western movies demonstrated this fact. Real men of honor fought with their fists, because it was nobler, somehow, to do so. If they used guns, size and strength were no longer of any particular advantage. In classic gun-slinger movies, speed with a gun replaced size and strength, but speed with a gun was still a physical skill. Any weapons that relied on stealth or craft were seen, in classic American mythology, as sneaky, disreputable, and unfair. Jud Fry, in *Oklahoma!*, is creepy because he threatens to use sneaky weapons—hidden knives and so on—instead of his bare fists, fair and square, in his conflict with Curly, the American hero. Sneaky weapons—concealed knives, poisons, and their kin—rob the American hero of his advantages: his strength, his courage, and his refusal to step away from a *fair* fight.

Magic is just such a weapon. Magic, when properly used, can be used at a distance, and can be used by the creepy, the sickly, the lame, and the incorporeal to vanquish the physically strong. The entire theme, if one can sum up such a sprawling universe with one theme, of Robert E. Howard's *Conan the Barbarian* stories is precisely this: the force of physical strength and courage, which is all Conan has, versus the sinister, tricky, unfair, and disembodied forces of magic and sorcery often wielded by physically unfit men or, even worse, women. Magic is an equalizing weapon, just like guns, and people who use it can be regarded with as much disdain as John Wayne once reserved for men who carried derringers.[*]

---

[*]We could make an exception for Harry Potter here, who is a widely beloved wielder of magic. But his creator knows that magicians are disreputable, too, as she demonstrates in every interaction Harry has with Muggles. And in the real world, Harry has many detractors as well, parents who see magicians as threats to civil and religious order. It is J. K. Rowling's genius that she creates a devalued category—Muggles—for real-world critics to step right into.

The average middle school, in this regard, is not unlike the Old West (at least the Old West of the movies, which is the only one we know). It is a complex society with members who are more or less valued but whose most valued members are admired because they embody the virtues that all members of the society value. This society is a version of adult American culture, but it is a caricature of it, because the people who inhabit it are not yet sensitive to subtle nuance. Kids in middle school admire physical size and strength in boys, and those boys who possess these attributes are valued accordingly. They are the natural aristocrats of the average middle school, and their continuing triumphs using size and strength, usually on the rule-bound playing fields but also in the un–rule-bound schoolyard, is what reinforces their aristocracy. Kids, especially boys, who cannot win on the playing field or in the schoolyard but who seek to win by using sneaky weapons are vilified because they undermine the whole American archetype. They are seen as lacking in courage and fairness; using magic is cheating.

Seen in this light, any kid who displays an interest in magic and fantasy is inherently subversive. Magic is for *losers,* in the concrete sense of the word: They cannot win by playing by the rules, so they have to resort to magic instead. Now, as adults know, an interest in magic and fantasy in the form of absorption in role-playing games is not the same as actually practicing magic, but these distinctions are not so clear-cut, especially when lived out in the archetypal preconsciousness of primitive thinkers. In the middle school world and, to a lesser extent, the high school world, all kids who are interested in equalizers are suspect. An interest in magic is suspect, and an interest in technology is suspect; technology is just an updated form of magic for those who find it mysterious. But the two together add up to one big creepy picture.

If this all sounds too Jungian for the average enlightened adult, one need only look at recent history for some stunning examples. The terrible incidents at Columbine High School in 1999 changed the world in many ways, but one of the most immediate ways was a nationwide persecution of Goths, nerds, geeks, and perceived misfits of all kinds. As eloquently described by the eminent social psychologist Elliot Aronson in his book *Nobody Left to Hate: Teaching Compassion After Columbine*, the nationwide panic that set in after Columbine had all the characteristics of a witch hunt: Parents and school officials alike were engaged in trying to identify a secret enemy hiding right there in our midst who had the motivation, and the capacity, to destroy our most precious possessions—our children. In this outbreak of paranoia, the three characteristics of the Columbine killers were brought together in mythic fashion: the Goth costumes, the technological sophistication (including the Internet boastings and the weapons), and the outcast and persecuted identity. What Columbine "taught" so many parents and teachers was easy to learn because the mythic underpinnings were already all present. What we "learned" was that unpopular kids are subjected to the unfortunate but expected and socially tolerated persecution by popular kids in high school, the aristocrats of the social order, and that when unpopular kids are persecuted, they may turn to some kind of equalizer to even the score. They may decide to break the rules, to try to take out the Curlys by using the tactics of Jud Fry. And, in this outbreak of paranoia, outcast kids all over the nation were identified by their weird fashions and their interest in technology and identified as the next potential killers.

It turns out that kids who are disturbed enough to kill their classmates are not so easily identified. The kids who killed or planned to kill their classmates in the immediate post-Columbine years were a pretty heterogeneous lot. They were all obviously unhappy, but certainly not all visibly or noticeably socially outcast or mercilessly teased. Since homicidal violence is such a low–base-rate phenomenon, prediction, as every psychologist knows, is an extremely dicey business. But identifying every Goth kid or every picked-on kid or every nerdy or geeky kid as a potential killer is a sure recipe for identifying a ton of false positives, to say the least. The post-Columbine Goth and geek persecution wasn't about reason or fact; it was about finding the Jud Frys who were planning to blow up the Curlys.

Popular culture tells us that a kid who starts to use magic is dangerous indeed. Magic, as an equalizer, can be used by girls as well as boys, and so girls can become sorceresses just like all those curvaceous and treacherous sorceress babes in the *Conan* stories. In contemporary pop fiction, the model for this is none other than our old friend Carrie, the eponymous antiheroine of Stephen King's breakthrough book. Carrie doesn't go looking for magic; she just discovers she has it. She is also greatly, widely, and deeply persecuted by her classmates, and she ultimately uses her magic powers in what may be described as the biggest revenge-of-the-nerds fantasy ever written: She kills every single one of her high school classmates at the senior prom when she is humiliated one too many times. Is it not at all surprising that *Carrie*, too, is on the ALA's list of the top one hundred challenged books of the years 1990 to 2000. *Carrie* demonstrates in operatic fashion what every kid and every parent "knows": Persecution of powerless kids works only when they're powerless. If, however, they somehow get a little power, watch out: The social order is about to be overturned. Whether or not this ever really happens is beside the point; the myths are just going on, being lived out, waiting to be evoked again and again by every new generation of kids.

GREAT PRETENDERS

Kids who are interested in magic are often not respected by other kids because, as we have seen, most mainstream kids think magic is for losers. But what do we think? Is there something about an interest in role-playing games that should worry us as adults? The question, from a grown-up point of view, has to do with compensatory fantasy. First of all, how do we know that fantasy or pretense on the part of kids beyond early elementary school is a compensation for something else? If magic is for losers, what have they lost at? And is it bad or unhealthy for kids to be interested in magic, even if it is compensatory? Over the years since its invention, many, many parents have militated against Dungeons & Dragons and have worried that it would somehow lead their kids astray, as if their kids' interest in these fantasy realms could cause mental or spiritual disease. Those parents seem to have given up, at least in an organized fashion. If they couldn't vanquish little old D&D, they don't stand a chance against Warhammer or World of Warcraft. But is there some truth in what nerd-labelers tell us: that magic is for losers or, worse yet, makes kids into losers?

When we consider this conclusion, we come up against another of those spectrum issues that so bedevil contemporary thinking on mental health. As we saw in chapter 4, the current view that mental illnesses lie at the end of a spectrum or a continuum from normal variation to frank mental illness is an enlightened view, but it also can lead to the overpathologizing of normal variation. In this case, we can certainly state that there is such a thing as too much involvement in compensatory fantasy. At the far end of the continuum, there is indeed something crazy—it's called being schizoid—but it is at the *far end* of the spectrum.

The term *schizoid* is similar to the term *schizophrenia*, and there is some overlap in symptoms, but it is not at all the same thing. A person is said to be in a schizoid state when he or she has withdrawn into a world of fantasy over which the subject has complete control. It is a state of disengagement from the real world and a state of almost complete engagement with a self-created world where the subject is, in effect, a god. Schizoid states can involve delusions when the person is so involved with the inner world that he or she loses the capacity to distinguish between fantasy and "reality," as defined by "consensual reality," or, in other words, what everybody else thinks is true. So there can be a fair amount of schizoid behavior in schizophrenia, or not so much, but it is perfectly possible to be in a schizoid state and not be psychotic: One can just be deeply preoccupied with the inner, self-created world and deeply uninterested in any other world, including the world we all live in.

People can go through their whole lives in a schizoid state. They usually don't have good relationships with real people, because they can't control real people the way they can in the fantasy world, but it is all a matter of degree. Fiction writers and playwrights and moviemakers, of course, all live at times in a semischizoid state: They are deeply involved in creating alternative realities. This is why Freud (incorrectly, in my view) viewed all artists with suspicion. If the task of growing up is to face reality dead on, without illusion, then creative artists are necessarily infantile or regressed to some degree. This is the big joke that Woody Allen, once popular culture's favorite analysand, tells over and over. In *Annie Hall*, for example, the character of Alvy Singer ends up writing a play in which his ex-girlfriend comes to her senses and comes back to him: As an artist, he is in complete control, and, in fantasy, he can make her do whatever he wants.

In grown-up life, then, people who pretend too much or spend too much time in a world of their own making are in some kind of trouble. The question is, how much trouble? One could comfortably rate all sorts of fantasy activities based on the level of schizoid withdrawal they demonstrate. Using such a scale, a man who spends all his time with his model railroad trains and model railroad village, a place over which he has complete control, is in more trouble than a teenager or adult who plays MMORPGs, because the latter activity has, by definition, multiple players. Success in a community of online orcs and wizards requires social skill, negotiating ability, and some kind of online equivalent of street smarts. Complete control is not at all what's happening; teamwork with allies or deadly interactions with enemies make omnipotent control, the hallmark of schizoid withdrawal, impossible. Just because it's in front of a keyboard doesn't make it schizoid.

Melissa, a smart and popular college student, laughs with me about this phenomenon when she talks about her concerns about her seventeen-year-old brother, Zack. She thinks Zack spends far too much time playing MMORPGs. Somehow, she thinks it's not healthy to spend so much time in front of the computer. Zack spends a lot of time playing World of Warcraft online, and she thinks he ought to be outside doing something "real." Recently when she called home, Zack wouldn't stay on the phone, because, he said, he was in the middle of a World of Warcraft maneuver: "I can't talk now, we're staging a raid," he said. So Melissa asked to speak to her mom. "She can't talk either," Zack told her. "She's in on the raid." So Zack is not alone in front of the computer after all: He's online, and mom, in another room, is also online, and they're staging a raid together.

How real is smashing dragons and saving the Realm of Azeroth with your mom? Really real or not at all real, depending on how you look at it. But how real would it be if Zack were playing soccer? More real? If there were goals and two competing teams and everyone was all pumped about who could get the ball into whose net? In terms of real-life consequences, it's not exactly earth-shattering; no one's life is going to be changed as a result of who gets the ball into whose net. True, if he were playing soccer, Zack would be getting some exercise and fresh air, but in terms of teamwork, heart-pumping excitement, and good clean fun, which activity is more real, soccer with the boys or World of Warcraft with Mom and several hundred other eager players all over the globe? Looks like a toss-up to me.

But I am not a kid. Kids, both boys and girls, lose interest in pretend play in the course of their development, and anyone who lingers too long in the dress-up corner becomes suspect. Ask any college-age LARPer (that's live-action role-playing game player, for those not fully acronymized). They don't use computers at all to play their games. They don't even use game boards or little homemade pieces. They use their own robes and capes and wooden swords and wands and talismans of all kinds. And fires . . . they like fires. They play outside, in the woods, in the fresh air, and they get plenty of exercise as they run around enacting the live-action avatars they have chosen for themselves. And believe me, the fresh air and physical activity and lack of computers does not spare them from being nerd- and geek-labeled. They are, in the eyes of their college classmates, as geeky as you can get. Pretending, this kind of pretending, is suspect because it is seen as childish, and nerds and geeks, as we have seen, are just one short step above "babies."

PRETENDING TO BE REAL

If we were going to try to figure out the whole compensatory fantasy thing, it would be nice to know which comes first, the social rejection or the preoccupation with magic and fantasy. Do kids who love magic and fantasy and linger a little too long in the world of make-believe get labeled as nerds and geeks because of their apparent immaturity? Or do kids get rejected, for whatever reason—maybe for their good grades in math or their closeness to adults—and then turn to fantasy and magic, the great equalizers, as a compensation? There are most probably a lot of both types, but is there a predominant theme in here waiting to be found?

Two decades ago, I tried to answer this question for myself. I was working as a researcher on a large-scale study of how to alleviate social isolation in late-elementary-school kids. We were working on various forms of intervention to see what worked to bring unpopular kids into the fold, so to speak, of their peers. This was not an easy job; we had to convince public schools to let us use standard psychological instruments to get kids to identify their most isolated peers, and many schools were understandably leery about opening this can of worms for their students. When we found schools to let us in, we used the classic tools of sociometry, measuring social networks, to figure out who was who, and then we tested various kinds of group interventions to help the kids on the fringes.

I was then, as I am now, distractible, and I found myself becoming much more interested in the kids' inner lives than I was in their social behavior. So I did a study looking at the fantasy lives of our subjects. We had identified children in three distinct social-status groups based on their peer ratings: a group of quietly isolated kids (what we might now call nerds and geeks, although, believe it or not, the terms were almost unknown in elementary schools twenty years ago), a group of aggressive kids who were socially marginalized, and a group of popular kids. We asked kids in all three groups to respond to the following question: If you could be a superhero and have one superpower, what would it be? The kids were invited to tell stories about their invented superheroes: the origin of their powers, their families, their exploits, and their secret identities, if any. Although it makes some kind of intuitive sense that kids in these three categories would be somehow different in their fantasy lives, predicting from inner life to outer life is never easy or clear-cut.

But there were differences, very clear differences. The aggressive marginalized kids chose, not surprisingly, explosive powers: They could "blow up anything in the world" or "shatter anything that moved" or have the power to "supersmash." The quietly isolated kids, the proto-nerds and geeks, were most likely by far to have the most magical powers. These kids chose two powers way more than any others: flying and being invisible. How come? Unfortunately, research like this, which looks at correlations and not causes, cannot answer the question for sure: I found which fantasies went with which kids but could not specify which came first, the social status or the inner life. It certainly seemed like the powers they chose were compensations, but it is worthy of note that these peer-isolated kids did not choose powers they might have used for revenge: They seemed to want powers that would just help them get away.

The findings of real interest were in the fantasy lives of the popular kids. These kids' superheroes were the least super of any superheroes ever. They chose powers like "the power to be the best cheerleader in the world" or "the power to be liked by everyone" or "the power to have the coolest car in the world." It was like these kids were just looking ahead to adolescence and describing what they thought would be cool about it. Their fantasy horizons, their ability and/or their willingness to pretend, was severely self-limited. This might have been because they didn't want to be seen pretending or doing anything babyish like make-believe. They did participate in making up the stories; they just didn't go very far in their imaginations.

How come? My subjects demonstrated pretty clearly that kids who are socially successful on the outside feel different on the inside as well. Kids who are popular in late elementary school are not popular because they're quirky; they're popular because they're as normal as they can be. And they participate in normality by seeing the next stage as continuous with this one: Why the heck do I need to be invisible? Why would I want to do that? I'm looking ahead to what is coming next for me: teenage popularity. If Warhammer had been around back then, these kids would never in a million years have been playing Warhammer. That kind of thing would have been just too weird for them. The weirdness of Warhammer is self-perpetuating, as is the normality of mainstream kids: "I wouldn't do Warhammer, because kids like me don't do Warhammer." Simple as that.

Researchers who study normality are always led into the same tautology, but here it is again. When you try to identify people who *are* psychologically normal, the one reliable thing that seems to distinguish them, above all else, is that they *define* themselves as normal. They squeeze out any and all weirdness, because they don't want it. To these aggressive mental centrists, nerds and geeks are not normal. They're just not. What else do they need to know? As we have seen, the nerd/geek stereotype is so heterogeneous that it's awfully hard to understand. It is some combination of school success, interest in precision, unself-consciousness, closeness to adults, and interest in fantasy—things that just don't hang together, conceptually or in real people. But to normal people, all these things are not normal; that's what all the components of the stereotype have in common. So maybe the best way to understand what nerdiness and geekiness are all about is to go all the way and study their opposites. To get to the heart of the geek, we need to go through the heart of the ungeek. Maybe the only way finally to understand Ichabod Crane is to understand Brom Bones.

9.

WELCOME TO MY PERSECUTION

· OR ·

WHY THE GEORGE BUSH– AL GORE CONTEST WAS A JUNGIAN'S DREAM

Gore's pencil neck tugs at my nerdy soul. I think the most lovable thing he has ever said can be found in a sentence in his 1992 book *Earth in the Balance: Ecology and the Human Spirit*. On page 67, he asks, "What happened to the climate in the Yucatán around 950?" Something about the specifics of that query lit me up. For the first time, I could see myself casting my ballot for a man who would pose such a question. It was just so boldly arcane.

So Sarah Vowell, in *The Partly Cloudy Patriot*, her brilliant, heartfelt book about American civic participation, described her passion for Al Gore in the 2000 presidential election—Al Gore, the man of ideas and, more important, the man of facts. Gore was, in 2000, the nerd archetype come to life: a guy who, first and foremost, did his homework. His mastery of the facts—of global warming, of international law, of the ins and outs of Washington, where he had spent most of his life—was seen by many as his primary qualification for the job of president. But Gore, the archetypal nerd, was up against something much bigger than George Bush in the election of 2000. Vowell continues:

> This is the Gore of the first presidential debate with Bush, the sighing, eye-rolling, eager beaver, buttinsky Gore, interrupting Bush to ask the moderator, Jim Lehrer, "Can I have the last word on this?" Ross G. Brown commented in the *Los Angeles Times*, "Gore studied hard and was thoroughly prepared for the televised civics and government quizzes each debate provided. A teacher might have given him an A. But much of the rest of the class just wanted to punch Mr. Smarty-Pants in the nose."

All true, way too true. But *why* did much of the rest of the class, and much of the rest of America, want to punch Mr. Smarty-Pants in the nose? What was it about Al Gore's erudition that was so annoying to so many people? It could not have been just the erudition. After all, as we have seen, Bill Clinton knew a hell of a lot of facts too, and he didn't keep the knowledge of those facts to himself, but he never seemed to be smug or too pleased with himself for knowing all those facts. He was the ur-wonk, the man who made the term "wonk" what it is today, because we all needed a term to describe someone as brainy as Clinton who was, at the same time, so manifestly unnerdy.

But something about Al Gore, as Vowell points out, was experienced by the press and then by the American people as an archetypal nerd, and therefore he was on the receiving end of all the hostility evoked by the nerd/geek stereotype. But what was it, what is it? He didn't look like a nerd. He did not, in fact, have a "pencil neck." He is actually kind of bulky. He certainly didn't look pale or skinny or wear clothes that didn't fit, and he didn't wear glasses. He also was, if press reports were to be believed, pretty comfortable with his body: He was reported to have been shaking his booty on the dance floor the very night he finally conceded defeat in the contested election of 2000, and his passionate public kisses of his attractive wife were the stuff of campaign-trail legend.

It is impossible, of course, to understand how Gore was so completely tarred with the nerd brush without understanding the archetypal standing of Gore's opponent. George W. Bush was, at that time, the all-American popular kid, the jock's jock, the regular guy whose ignorance of facts was noted by the press (as in, for example, his inability to name foreign leaders on the campaign trail and his famous malapropisms) but was never held against him by the press or by the public. Vowell is hilarious on this point, describing Bush as the candidate "running for national gym teacher." He had a historic association with the world of sports, having been part owner of a baseball team. As president, he was famous for his exercise workouts, his brush-clearing on his ranch, and his vanity about his weight: every time he had his annual physical, and gained even a pound, the White House went to great pains to describe it as "muscle weight." *Compared with Gore*, Bush certainly looked like a jock.

But on closer inspection, how jocky was Bush? One might ask how the man ever retained his reputation as a jock when his major athletic accomplishment in high school was being a male cheerleader. Indeed, one might argue that the Democratic Party demonstrated once and for all its high-mindedness, as well as its stupidity, by not plastering the high school picture of George W. Bush with his pompoms on every billboard and television commercial in the country during the elections of 2000 and 2004. A male cheerleader, although associated with athletic endeavor, is not exactly the same thing as a jock. But this biographical fact, which would have killed off Gore or John Kerry in a heartbeat—and as awful as recent campaign propaganda has been, can you imagine what would have been made of a high school picture of John Kerry in a cheerleader's outfit?—never seemed to touch George W. Bush. How come?

Because there is something archetypal about the nerd–jock struggle that transcends real individuals. Now, in invoking the term *archetype*, which has both a technical meaning in Jungian psychology and a broader, more metaphorical meaning, we are marching into the fog. The term is slogged around carelessly, in its adjective form serving sometimes to refer to size, as a synonym for *titanic*, and sometimes to refer to history, as a synonym for *classic*. But *archetypal*, in its technical Jungian sense, refers to the evocation by figures in consciousness of constellations of desires and capabilities that are both universal and unconscious. Certainly the Bush–Gore struggle, like every jock-versus-nerd confrontation, seems to have the quality of an archetypal struggle. But it is not necessarily a struggle between archetypal figures; it's the struggle *itself* that is archetypal. In this sense, Gore is necessarily nerdy because we "know" that his opponent, Bush, is a jock; Gore's nerdity is necessitated by

Bush's jockity. And just as inevitably, we "know" that Bush is a jock because his adversary Gore is a nerd; Bush's jockity is a necessary complement to Gore's nerdity. It is the struggle, the opposition, that feels inevitable, and the real-life characteristics of the antagonists disappear or are given disproportionate weight to make them fit what we think we know about the struggle. This is why the usually accurate Scott Simon on NPR could refer to the steroid hearings on Capitol Hill as a "nerd versus jock" confrontation, when in fact many people in politics are there only because of their initial appeal and name recognition as jocks (Senator John Thune of South Dakota, for example, or Senator George Allen of Virginia). If there are jocks on one side, and it's a confrontation, *the other side, by definition, has to be nerds.*

Of course, if the nerd–jock struggle is "archetypal," one has to think about the nature of the archetypes. In Jung's description of archetypes, they are weirdly specific: the *anima*, for example, is a pretty complicated constellation of unconscious wishes, talents, and ultimate goals, with four developmental levels corresponding to qualities associated with women in mythology and religion (Eve, Helen, Mary, and Sophia). If we were looking for the archetypes that are universal, unconscious, and always in opposition that might be the psychic urtext for the nerd–jock struggle, I suppose we could choose "the body" represented by jocks and "the mind" represented by nerds. But this isn't saying much. For one thing, in a real Jungian archetypal struggle, the antagonists would be given equal psychic weight and desirability. The nerd–jock struggle is weighted too heavily on the side of jocks to be an archetypal representation of a universal struggle between mind and body.

Perhaps it would be better to jettison the archetypes. After all, they are supposed to reflect universal human tendencies, and, as we have seen, the nerd–jock struggle that feels so inevitable here is not so inevitable in other parts of the world. Maybe the Bush–Gore struggle, i.e., the jock–nerd struggle, is simply a new avatar of the American struggle between the Man of Action and the Man of Reflection (described in chapter 3), a struggle with deep historical roots. In this sense, Bush and Gore in 2000 could just have easily been Jackson and Jefferson, right down to the suspicions about "Old Europe." As Vowell notes in her brief history of the campaign,

> If *Newsweek*'s Jonathan Alter is correct, Bush's jockish disdain for highbrow thought is the very origin of his White House bid. "In a 1998 *New Yorker* piece [about Al Gore]," Alter claims, "the vice president talked about the ideas of Maurice Merleau-Ponty, a French existentialist. Bush read the article, and later told friends it was one of the reasons he ran for president—to keep intellectual pretentiousness out of the White House."

The fact that Bush's resolve could have been formed in 1828 may be one of the reasons it made sense to Bush's friends or supporters in 2000, but even this passage highlights some facts and downplays others. For one thing, since when does a jock like George W. Bush read *The New Yorker*? Isn't that Gore's territory? Bush went on to be elected and reelected, of course, and by the year 2006 he was proudly announcing his summer reading list, which included *The Stranger* by Albert Camus. Not surprisingly, he was promptly ridiculed in the national press; rather than see his newfound interest in French existentialism as a promising development, most commentators dismissed it as posturing. The argument seemed to be that Bush campaigned and got elected as an anti-European American Man of Action; that's who he *is*. For him to break out of that straitjacket was impossible to imagine. Sorry, George, jocks are not allowed to be nerds, and nerds are not allowed to be jocks. And if Michael Dukakis, in the presidential campaign of 1988, was ridiculed for appropriating military imagery that didn't fit with his nerdy image, then George W. Bush is not allowed to read Camus. Whether or not Bush really read or enjoyed Camus is beside the point; the point is, it is the straitjacket that feels inevitable.

But what about our current president? The election of 2008 was hard to make into a jock-versus-nerd contest, mostly because John McCain, while a former action hero, was too old and too prickly to be cast credibly as a jock. Barack Obama certainly had, and has, some makings of a nerd stereotype: he was described as "professorial" before the election, and since the election, the adjectives "dispassionate," "cool," and "technocratic" are piling up around him like tar balls on a Gulf Coast beach. But Obama is black, and, as everyone "knows," nerds are white guys. Obama is also an accomplished basketball player, so it is hard to describe him as a bodyless brain.

That hasn't stopped people from trying. The always irksome Joel Stein, writing in the *Los Angeles Times* in the run-up to the 2008 election, tried to cast Obama as none other than Steve Urkel, America's first black nerd, from the once popular comedy series *Family Matters*. The label didn't stick then. But it has reappeared recently in the discourse of the Tea Party movement. Steve Urkel was famous for his clumsiness: he often unintentionally broke things in spectacular fashion, and then looked around and said, in his trademark whine, "Did I do that?" Tea Partiers now sport placards at their protest rallies featuring Urkel bodies with pasted-on Obama heads with captions like "Trillion-dollar deficits . . . did I do that?" It remains to be seen whether or not this will stick, but for many in contemporary politics any form of character assassination is always worth a try.

The nerd-versus-jock straitjacket imposed on our national culture is, in fact, a big version of the straitjacket that all our children encounter as they approach middle school. The straitjacket doesn't fit right away; it takes a while to grow into. As we have seen, the nerd/geek stereotype is not immediately comprehensible to our kids, and they need a fair amount of indoctrination to get it at all. But when they begin to be indoctrinated, they get messages that are awfully confusing. Nerds are kids who are too goody-goody, like Boy Scouts, but they are also weird and sick, like kids with Asperger's syndrome who murder their classmates. Nerds are kids who are close to their parents and who are protected and cared for by adults but who also don't wash or use deodorant and have no idea how they are supposed to look, like kids brought up in orphanages. Nerds are too interested in details and arcane knowledge, except when those details are about something like fly-fishing. People who like those kinds of details are not nerds. Nerds are too interested in facts. They are too literal and scientific, except when they are too interested in fantasy or magic or alternate realities. It's no wonder kids are confused and sometimes get it wrong.

But maybe the one thing that is clear in all this is that nerdiness is not its opposite. As we have seen, little kids learn that nerds are bad. Indeed, the first thing that kids learn about nerds it that they are bad. So maybe the ultimate definition of nerdity is that it is everything that the good thing, the opposite thing, is not. To understand what it means to be a nerd, all you need to do is to understand what a nerd isn't.

This is actually very close to what kids actually experience. Because "nerd" is a devalued stereotype, most kids don't think of themselves as nerds until someone calls them a nerd. Then they have to consider what a nerd is and whether or not they are one. But the act of knowledge, or self-knowledge, is prompted by an act of exclusion that is set in motion by one kid, saying to another, "You're a nerd." Translation: "You are a devalued member of this community, or you are no longer in the community. You're outside the pale." Kids don't spontaneously wake up one morning and ask themselves "Am I a nerd?" or "Am I a geek?" any more than adults spontaneously muse on the question "Am I an asshole?" The only reason to ask oneself the question is that the name has been laid at one's door, actually or by association. Someone might call me as asshole for driving an SUV, or might, in my presence, call someone else an asshole for driving an SUV; in either case, if I drive an SUV, I might have to consider whether or not I'm an asshole. Without the stimulus, however, the question might not occur to me just out of the blue. In the same manner, when kids are faced with this act of exclusion, they can try to puzzle out what it means to be a nerd, which isn't all that easy. Or they might try to understand it by understanding the community from which they have just been excluded.

This is not all conscious, and it can happen in an instant, but when it does, it can be very powerful. Consider the following exchange, reported to me by a reserved, studious young male acquaintance named Angus. This conversation happened when Angus was in the eighth grade, between him and a kid he barely knew, in the hallway at his school:

KID: "Hey, Angus, are you a virgin?"
ANGUS: "Yeah. Like you're not."
KID: "You know what? You're not as nerdy as I thought you were."

Now, as conversation goes, this is pretty complicated stuff, the kind of conversation that drives artificial-intelligence people wild because it is so impossibly human and therefore so difficult for a computer to generate or understand. But let's unpack it. Kid implies an insult, and in retrospect implies that Angus is a nerd for being a virgin. Angus demonstrates, by his reply, that he (a) is quick-witted, (b) knows that most eighth-graders are virgins no matter what they might pretend, and (c) is not easily bullied. Whereupon Kid says, "I was going to call you a nerd for being a virgin, but now, even though you are in fact a virgin, I am not going to call you a nerd because you have demonstrated by your reply that you are not." So how did Angus demonstrate that he is not? It can't be (a), can it? Nerds are notoriously quick-witted. So it must be (b) or (c), probably (c). In either case, this is not the kind of question that shows up on an "Are you a nerd?" self-test; it's way too subtle. But not being easily pushed around, not being rattled or anxious when attacked—this might be just the sort of thing that really separates the nerds from the . . . let's see, what are we going to call them?

VOX POPULI

I guess "pops"—what most kids call "the popular kids"—is a term as good as any. Every kid in every school knows who they are, and every kid in every school (at least every middle school) wants to be one of them. The pops are an odd bunch: If you ask kids why some kids are pops and not others, they can't really tell you. For most middle school kids, popular kids just *are*, like mountains or parents or air, and popular kids don't know any more about this than nonpops. In my time as a researcher on children's social development, I spent a lot of time asking pops why they were pops, and they had absolutely no idea. Many of them, in fact, did not feel like pops, and they spent just as much time as everyone else, maybe even more, worrying about their social status—the middle school social equivalent of what Barbara Ehrenreich has called "fear of falling."

But the one thing pops have mastered is the appearance of being at ease, no matter what their internal panic. These are the kids who have mastered pseudo–self-consciousness: Somehow, they know exactly what they are expected to do, and they do it. They are normal, regular, and, most of all, superficially genial. They are sometimes mean (see below) but much of the time, pops are extraordinarily genial. The two things they know really well is how to get along with others and how to deflect criticism.

The other thing that a lot of pops know is how to persecute nerds and geeks. Now, it is true that students of children's peer relationships will point out that the truly worst persecutors— the "mean girls" and their male equivalents—are not the most popular kids but those one or two or even three rungs down the ladder of social success who are trying to move up. The phenomenon is sadly familiar in the world of adults: For example, we have recently arrived immigrants who are most vociferous about excluding newer immigrants, or (in my neck of the woods) recently arrived migrants to the bucolic countryside militating against any new growth that would let in a new batch of ex-urbanites. Status anxiety always makes people eager to "kiss up and kick down," and children's peer groups are no exception.

The unthinkingness of the phenomenon is what makes children's peer groups so extraordinary, when perceived through adult eyes. Take the example of Bart, a popular, athletic kid who was the natural aristocrat of his middle school, and whose put-downs of the nerdy and geeky around him were legendary for their wittiness and brutality. Imagine, if you will, a sort of twelve-year-old jock with the tongue of Oscar Wilde. When Bart's star was fading, when he was in high school, he began to be the object of revenge. All sorts of kids he had put down began rejecting him with the same energy, if not the same talent, he had used against them years earlier. But Bart was completely undone by this. He remembered having rejected and scorned a lot of kids, but he could not for the life of him remember why. It just seemed, to him, like the thing to do or the thing that was required of him. He had no memory of being nasty, and when he was reminded of having been very nasty to particular kids, he could hardly believe it. "Why would I have done that?" he would ask me, as if I knew. "There's nothing wrong with that kid." If there was ever a kid who might convert a therapist to the dark paths of Jungian psychology, Bart was that kid. It was as if he had been overtaken by something much bigger than himself in an almost avolitional fashion. And years later, he was both apologetic and dazed, as though the visiting archetype had finally decided to move on to its next victim.

In this light, the struggle between Bush and Gore in 2000 was not a jock-versus-nerd struggle; it was an archetypal pop-versus-nerd struggle. There were two people, real people, who represented different points of view, but they all got swept up in a mythic struggle that was in some ways thrust upon them both. The nature of this sweeping was evident in how they handled, and were handled by, the press. In Sarah Vowell's account, she noted the contribution of the press to the Gore = nerd equation:

> Writing about a man who knows so much and who isn't shy about sharing his knowledge must have gotten on a lot of journalists' nerves. Recalling Gore's press conferences, Eric Pooley of *Time* wrote, "Whenever Gore came on too strong, the room erupted in a collective jeer, like a gang of 15-year-old Heathers cutting down some helpless nerd."

We may wonder why these supposedly enlightened members of the fourth estate acted this way. But it was clear that Al

Gore was undone by this treatment, while George W. Bush, being a pop, knew *exactly* how to handle it. He took influential members of the press and gave them all nicknames. And they all, apparently, fell fawning at his feet like the wannabes they revealed themselves to be.

The nickname thing, reported widely in the early years of the Bush administration, went something like this: Everybody, no matter how potentially hostile, got a cute nickname especially made up for them by the commander-in-chief, who used these nicknames on the Washington press corps time and time again, just like he used cute nicknames on his inner circle. By calling Dick Keil of Bloomberg News "Stretch," and Bill Sammon of *The Washington Times* "Superstretch," and Candy Crowley of CNN "Dolce," Bush made these straight-A students feel like they were just like Scooter, and Rummy, and Turd Blossom, and all the rest of the White House fraternity. The same belligerent Washington press corps who had seethed with resentment when Gore showed off his superior knowledge apparently went into a swoon when they got their nicknames, and stopped asking hard questions for about the next five years.

Speaking as a good student and former dictionary, I can attest to the seductive power of nicknames. I have always been called David, and hardly ever anything else. Some of the more adventurous members of my immediate family call me Dave, but that's as far as it goes. With a last name like Anderegg, a nickname like Andy would be a natural, but no one has ever even breathed it in my direction. I remember being stunned when I went to a bar with a particularly sociable uncle and heard all the patrons calling him Andy. Wow! How did he do that? Well, he probably did something I have never done: He probably said, "Call me Andy." Somehow, overtly or covertly, he gave people permission to call him a nickname, and they did. It's not rocket science, but it somehow never occurs to rocket scientists, or to a lot of intelligent but socially reserved people who might envy the easy familiarity implied by nicknames but never seem to figure out how to get one.

Popular kids always have nicknames. Even when the nicknames are insulting (and I can't believe that Karl Rove doesn't, somewhere in his mischievous soul, object to being called "Turd Blossom"), pops are not insulted by them. The laid-back informality is not a cause but a sign of the natural social ease that made people love George W. Bush and distrust Al Gore, who apparently is a very nice guy but never quite seems to be a naturally nice guy. Being naturally at ease, being happy with oneself in one's own skin, is the quality that makes everyone else go all mushy inside. As some political commentators, especially Paul Krugman of *The New York Times*, have noted of late, the W presidency did not turn out particularly well, and some may have learned to regret voting for a president whose best quality, compared with the traits of his opponents in both elections, seemed to be his natural ease with himself, his own lovable self-love.

Self-confidence is always appealing, or almost always appealing, especially so to people who have very little of it, that is, kids in middle school. It seems to go something like this: Somewhere around the time kids start to reach the beginnings of puberty—real puberty, that is, not the pseudo-puberty of tween marketing—some kids are designated as pops. They don't ask for this designation, and they have no idea why it is conferred upon them. Usually it is conferred because these kids are the most normal in appearance: They have no defects, and they seem to embody the virtues that everybody wants to have. And when they get designated as pops, and the more pop they are, the most at ease they feel. In other words, the popularity seems to be both naturally occurring and socially conferred: Kids who seem to be kind of normal, cute, and uncontroversial are elected as pops by the consent of the governed. And thereafter, they are treated with respect and deference, which makes them more confident and even more appealing. Conversely, kids who are weird or unpop or nerdy or geeky get treated with contempt and feel less confident; therefore they seem less appealing, at least while everyone is under the spell that lasts until later in high school. Then most kids wake up and realize that variety is the spice of life, and nerd/geek persecution abates dramatically.

MUTTON AND LAMB

Or does it? It would be lovely to say that as kids get more flexible and more secure after having negotiated the rocky shoals of puberty, the American ideal begins to mature. The self-loving normal pop kid is completely understandable as the ideal middle school citizen. And if you talk to high school kids, you know that as they mature they start to act as if worshipping pops and vilifying nerds and geeks is sort of, well, middle-schoolish.

So why do we still valorize pops as adults? Why does it seem that the American ideal is still mired in the mind of an eleven-year-old? Why did the political press corps and the American public vote for someone whose major asset was his affability? Why is it that, if you start paying attention, you see daily evidence of competent grown-ups being punished for their nerdiness and apparently sane and mature people citing "attractiveness" or social grace or self-love as an asset to be prized above every other asset?

Let's go to the evidence, shall we? In one short period in late winter of 2007, *The New York Times* informed us of the following current events:

The Delta Zeta Massacre. A psychology professor at DePauw University in Indiana did an on-campus survey to assess the reputations attached to various fraternities and sororities, and in that survey the Delta Zeta house girls were labeled by their classmates as "socially awkward." So the honchettes from the national chapter of Delta Zeta moved in and expelled every girl who was not a pop. All the black, Korean, and Vietnamese girls got the ax. So did all the overweight girls. So did all the nerdy girls. The Delta Zeta girls were obviously devoted to each other, something one would think would be highly valued in a sorority experience. One girl interviewed by the *Times* lamented, "I had a sister I could go to a bar with if I had boy problems. I had a sister I could talk about religion with. I had a sister I could be nerdy about science with. That's why I liked Delta Zeta, because I had all these amazing women around me." But they all got asked to leave, except for the twelve girls who were "slender and popular with fraternity men—conventionally pretty women the sorority hoped could attract new recruits." Six of those remaining girls quit in protest, God bless 'em. The faculty interviewed noted that the expelled girls were "less about image and more about academic achievement and social service."

The Asian Pop-Music Blackball. The *Times* Sunday Styles section did a story in honor of Paul Kim, the cool popular singer with the great voice who was sent packing as soon as America started to vote on the hit TV show *American Idol.* There was no apparent reason for Kim to be sent off the show so soon, except the obvious reason: his ethnicity. There are no Asian-American popular music stars, none whatsoever. How could that be, in a popular culture that celebrates diversity in every way imaginable? The *Times* says, "People in the music industry, including some executives, have no ready explanation, but Asian-American scholars and artists argue that the racial stereotypes that hobble them as a group—the image of the studious geek, the perception that someone who looks Asian must be a foreigner—clash with the coolness and born-in-the-USA authenticity required for American pop stardom." In other words, Asians cannot be popular-music stars not because of their Asianness primarily but because their Asianness makes people think of them as "studious geeks," and therefore . . . unpopular, I suppose one would have to say. Trying for coolness? No geeks need apply: America knows that geeks cannot be cool, by definition.

The Likable-President Recurring Nightmare. David Brooks, the sort-of-conservative columnist for the *Times,* wrote a piece on the sterling qualities of Bill Richardson, the former New Mexico governor and congressman and UN ambassador who is a dark-horse candidate hoping to be nominated by the Democratic Party to be its presidential candidate. Brooks mocks the Democrats for their penchant for nominating unlikable candidates, noting that "once a century or so the Democratic Party actually nominates somebody the average person would like to have a beer with. Bill Richardson is that kind of guy." This quality of Richardson's might actually turn out to be important. But is David Brooks, presumably a responsible or at least not totally deranged observer of the political scene, actually saying this sort of thing in 2007? Yo, David: Can you say Iraq? Katrina? Walter Reed? Maybe, just maybe, the affability and the "I'd like to have a beer with"—ness of the guy is not the thing most needed right now. We had one of those affable, self-loving guys. Can we really afford to have another one, to sit around and have a beer with another president while the ship of state runs even further aground?

The pop-versus-nerd struggle makes perfect sense in middle school. But the foregoing examples all involve people far beyond the eighth grade. What we see, if we read the newspapers, is that perfectly nice and supportive sorority sisters are unwanted, because they might be nerdy or unpop. We see that perfectly great Asian singers are unwanted, because they are way too geeky to have around. And we see that perfectly smart and experienced presidential candidates are devalued because they do not seem to have the easy self-love that we apparently require in a president. Hostility toward nerds and geeks wastes a lot of human capital and impoverishes everyone in the process.

But why are so many of us still stuck in middle school? The several explanations that come to mind all revolve around the same theme: anxiety. Anxiety is what makes mature people who should be thinking like nuanced, sophisticated grown-ups think instead like middle school kids, who have the excuse of immaturity. Anxiety is what makes people think that there are only two choices to be made. We might, then, take a look at what Americans, or at least some Americans, are so anxious about now, in order to see what kind of quiet desperation makes people feel so determined to perpetuate rigid stereotypes of what people can and cannot be.

A big factor here is hipness, and the terrible anxiety most Americans now face about being irrelevant because of their age. Part of this is due, of course, to mass marketing: Since marketers in general wish to score with younger consumers whose brand loyalties are not yet written in stone, popular culture is skewed toward the young. Movies, certainly, seem more and more designed to appeal to the tastes of teenagers, and television shows that score with older audiences are often neglected by the advertisers who pay the bills. Finding a way to stay young and hip and connected to the youthful energy of the market is the Holy Grail of much of American consumerism. So getting old is pretty scary if one wants to stay employed. Looking young, acting young, and especially thinking young are increasingly vital in a society where youth, in all its energy and variety, is an object of worship. Another part of the driving force behind youth worship is demographic: As baby boomers age and reproduction rates fall, young people become a more and more valued commodity. Aging cities fall all over themselves trying to prove they are hip places to live, and cities that are seen as "old and cold" desperately attempt to prove otherwise so that they do not lose the educated young people they need to stay competitive and vital in the future.

In such an environment, it is not surprising that older people do not act their age; they want to seem like they are thinking young. And as we have seen, nerdity is, in many senses, defined by the degree to which kids identify with the wishes of older people. Nerd-labeled kids do their homework, work on their merit badges, go to church or synagogue, and are often much closer to their parents than nerd-labeling kids. Popularity among peers is often defined in opposition to the world of adults, and kids who are compliant or "goody-goody" are precisely the kids who are labeled as socially undesirable. Valuing what adults value is what gets you labeled in the first place, so one of the things that has to go, in order to avoid social death, is compliance with adult expectations of good behavior.

But when you grow up, you're supposed to change. You're supposed to start to value, nay, insist on things like hard work, minding your manners, turning things in on time, cleanliness, citizenship, and all those things. That is what adults are supposed to do: help civilize people and help them learn how to be upright. But in a culture that valorizes youth and hipness at all costs, acting like a grown-up is too much like "thinking old." Instead of acting one's age, one can act younger than one's age by assuming the snarkiness of the young and dumping on nerds and geeks the way people do when they really are young.

This may be one reason why nerd and geek stereotypes persist when other stereotypes are fading. Adults do not condone racial stereotypes, and when kids use them, they usually run into a heap of trouble from the adults in charge. Racial epithets, and now even antigay slurs, are roundly condemned by adults, and kids learn very quickly that the way to get into a lot of trouble is to demonstrate that kind of unthinking prejudice when adults are around. But adults allow, and give voice to, antinerd prejudices all the time. It is simply amazing to encounter the number of adults who reify this stereotype in front of their kids by deriding their schoolmates as nerds and geeks. It is a completely acceptable stereotype in most social circles. Even people who bear all the visible stigmas of nerdiness will go out of their way to assert that they are "really" not nerds rather than to assert that "nerd" is not a useful or socially acceptable way to talk about people.

But hipness is a cruel mistress. Dumping on nerds and nerdity, or apologizing for one's apparent nerdity as if it were a runny nose, is vital if one is going to try to pretend to be young. The fact that this is undignified is beside the point; dignity is also pretty much out if one wants to seem young. The cutting British idiom for this kind of thing, usually used in the context of fashion, is "mutton dressed up like lamb." It is undignified to be an older person trying to pretend to be young. And in the context of nerd/geek stereotypes, we see a tremendous number of older Americans pretending to be younger than they really are. Al Gore's biggest crime, in the eyes of the Washington press corps, was his unhip embrace of the climate of the Yucatán and his even unhipper refusal to notice that other people would not be impressed with such knowledge. But the press corps' snarky disdain for Gore was a lot of mutton dressing up like a lot of lamb: people trying to claim the mantle of youth by being contemptuous of the mantle of authority that goes with doing your homework.

And so we come full circle, back to the young American nation, because the other part of the Man of Action–Man of Reflection dichotomy was the emphasis on the youth and vigor of the American nation, compared with the musty, ossified, plain old ways of Europe (sometimes known as "Old Europe"). America was a young country back then, and the valorization of youth above everything else was something, well, new. Now, however, the split between the old and musty and the new and fresh is internal, so to speak. It's not between America and Europe anymore; it's between Old America and New America. The old and musty is still the territory of the nerds and geeks, just like it was in Ichabod Crane's time, but what is the territory of the new, the young, the fresh? Since everyone is so terrified of being old, or of being seen as old, the only choice is to dress up like lamb, and that means, above all, being *irreverent*. If there's anything that characterizes pops, in their middle school and early-high-school heyday, it is their irreverence for the things that adults want them to revere: studying, classical music, algebra . . . anything "harrrd." And the big reason that so much of the adult world looks like pops gone wild is precisely that: No one, at least in the highly visible world of popular culture, wants to revere anything for fear of appearing to be a mossback. Reverence is for the old . . . and you know what that gets you: a pink slip and premature retirement.

If this analysis is correct, we can look forward to a lot more nerd-bashing in the future. Because as children get more and more scarce, and we need to do whatever we can to keep them around, we certainly can't rely on dignity or maturity to do it. Better go with snarky and juvenile, and hope they won't notice that we're really mutton and not lamb. The problem is, they always do notice; teenagers and college students and young adults of all kinds can smell desperation just as well as anyone else—maybe even better, because they have so much practice. Imitating and modeling the worst of middle school doesn't convince anyone that we're young and hip anyway, so maybe it's time to give dignity another try.

CONCLUSION:
THE NERD YOU SAVE

D yan is seventeen. She is an excellent student, a talented cellist, and a self-labeled geek. She has a close
group of friends, and they call themselves the Geek Club.
They laugh about their geeky tribe, but they have a strict membership requirement: One has to have taken calculus in order
to join. She does not and has almost never watched television, and she wouldn't know the difference between Ashton
Kutcher and Brad Pitt.

Lara, thirteen, who lives in the next town and is also an
excellent student, plays soccer and hangs out with a varied
group of friends. She recently confessed to her mother that
she has been dogging it on math bees at school, because she
won so many in a row that kids were starting to tease her about
being "geeky." She is a devotee of *Beauty and the Geek*, even
though her mother tells her it is garbage. She tells her mom
that "it's all fake," that nobody really acts like those people,

that none of it is real, and therefore her mom shouldn't worry about whether she will be influenced by the show.

These two kids are just two kids; their two stories represent just two of all the complex ways kids interact with nerd/geek stereotypes. But as we try to think about whether or not to be worried about the effects of these stereotypes, they might suggest to us who is in trouble and who is not. Dyan is not in trouble; like thousands of nerd-labeled kids, she laughs it off now, at seventeen. Her family is not exactly mainstream, and she will go on to an adult life like theirs: a scientific or technical job, and marriage to a lovely person who will probably also be a formerly nerd-labeled adult. We don't need to worry about the Dyans of the world or the Bill Gateses or the Esther Dysons.

We do need to worry about the Laras, however. There are a whole lot of kids driving down the middle of this highway, and they could go either way. They could decide to realize their talents, ignore social pressures, and risk doing things they are good at even if it gets them labeled as nerds or geeks. Or they could dog it, decide that math is too "harrrd," and tell themselves that it doesn't matter how well they do in math or science, because it's a relief not to have to worry about being nerd-labeled. Then, when they are out of school, they will be one of the forty-eight percent of young adults who tell researchers they wish they had taken more advanced math classes in high school.

We don't know this for certain, of course. As we have seen, there is almost no research on the issue of nerd/geek stereotypes and their effects on kids' actual performance in school. But we can extrapolate from other bodies of research. Research about the effects of television violence, for example, tells us what common sense suggests: Television violence doesn't make healthy kids violent. Kids who are grounded, feel loved, and probably don't watch that much TV anyway aren't going to go out and shoot someone if they see it on TV. But kids who are already vulnerable for other reasons, like family disorganization or neglect or other emotional difficulties, can be pushed off a cliff by exposure to violent television programs. In similar fashion, we might expect that kids with great ego strength and supportive families might be annoyed by being called nerds or geeks, but they won't suffer any long-lasting damage, except perhaps a long-lasting antipathy for alpha dogs.

The kids who will really be hurt by nerd/geek stereotypes are the kids who will shut down parts of themselves in order to fit in. These are the kids in the middle, who could go either way, but don't seem to be going the nerd way. As we have seen, math and science achievement in schools keeps dropping, and math and science majors in college are disappearing. It doesn't require a rocket scientist to suggest that there might be a link between a virulently anti-intellectual, and especially antiscientific, popular culture and the alarming diminution of science literacy among American kids.

CHANGING A CULTURE

As it turns out, the rocket scientists are busy suggesting remedies, but cultural change is not one of them. A brief look at the recent spate of studies of America's science literacy will reveal an astonishing unanimity of opinion. To a person, researchers cite the urgent need to compete that was sparked by the launching of the Soviet Union's Sputnik satellite in 1957. Everyone felt then that America had to do something to catch up, and we did. But to the chagrin of the blue-ribbon panels that study such things, the American public does not feel such urgency now, even though the issues are not much different: Advisory commissions from the Sputnik era recognized the anti-intellectual attitudes of American kids and called for action to change those attitudes in order to increase American competitiveness. But today's advisory panels, while acknowledging the cultural problems affecting science literacy, seem to have thrown in the towel on cultural change as if the attitudes of Americans can't possibly be budged.

Take, for example, the final report from the Committee on Science, Engineering, and Public Policy, a joint venture made up of members from the National Academy of Sciences, the National Academy of Engineering, and the Institute of Medicine. Their report, *Rising Above the Gathering Storm: Energizing and Employing America for a Brighter Economic Future*, which came out in 2005, is filled with alarming statistics about the state of American education and the economic consequences in the near future for America's global competitiveness. It is also filled with passing observations about American culture: Jeffrey Immelt, the CEO of General Electric, is quoted as saying that we're basically doomed because, in 2004, we graduated more sports-exercise majors from U.S. colleges than we did electrical engineers. But the remedies suggested, not surprisingly, are all about economic incentives, not about cultural change. The blue-ribbon panelists suggest we need to spend more to train teachers, to encourage teachers to be better, and to add economic incentives (like scholarships for AP exams in science and math) to help kids choose advanced science education.

But given the vital importance of this matter to every business leader on the planet, why is there not even any *research* on cultural factors? The approach of policy makers to attitude change seems to be indirect, through incentivization, in reports like *Rising Above the Gathering Storm*. But what good will $100 incentives do in high school when kids have already been brainwashed in middle school, if not before, to believe that no one who does well in science or math will ever get laid? Pretend that you are a teenager and you make the choice: A $100 scholarship and a lifetime of sexual abstinence? Or a D in math and a reputation for being cool and all that goes with it? What'll it be? I know which one I'd choose, and I think I know which one all those kids in the middle of the highway of life are choosing: They're taking the exit marked "Love—Dead Ahead."

Changing popular culture is not easy. It requires, first, a recognition on the part of a majority of people that the popular culture needs to be changed. The best modern example of this is antismoking propaganda, which is innovative, well financed, and relentless in its efforts to convince kids that smoking is not a good idea. But the motivation—decades of research that demonstrates that smoking really kills people—is there to provide the motivation to support all that propaganda. Cultural change about nerd/geek stereotypes may take a while. We don't have the research yet to prove what seems too obvious to need proving: that nerd/geek stereotypes, while not lethal, might be permanently impoverishing.

But wait! You might say, especially if you're an Ashton Kutcher fan, *Beauty and the Geek* is not about rigid stereotypes; it's about positive transformation! The geeks get less geeky, and the beauties get smarter! They decide who wins by deciding who has come the farthest in his or her "personal journey." The "nerd transcended" theme should provide the cultural change we might really need, right? Isn't Kutcher actually undermining the whole geek thing, and shouldn't he be applauded for it?

And what about Disney's *High School Musical*, the televised musical comedy that is the most popular entertainment ever among tweens? It, too, features the "nerd transcended" theme. The high school jock and the high school "Einsteinette" both try out for the high school musical and move beyond the narrow confines of their rigidified social roles as they sing about "breakin' free"! What could be a more positive, liberating message? Isn't this what cultural change is all about?

Well, no, actually. There is some relevant research on this topic, although it is not about the deleterious effects of nerd/geek stereotypes. It's the research on what social psychologists call "pluralistic ignorance": the tendency to overestimate the bad things a peer group is doing and then to take that as the norm and imitate it. Pluralistic ignorance is the phenomenon that explains why so many public-service campaigns about bad behavior don't work with adolescents or young adults; they just teach kids how to be bad. Many college anti–binge-drinking campaigns have failed for this reason. These failed campaigns have two basic messages: (1) What most kids do on this campus is binge-drink; and (2) You shouldn't. But the freshmen at whom these campaigns are targeted are so desperate to fit in that they pay attention only to the first message: Kids here binge-drink. . . . Okay, I guess I better do that, too, because that's the done thing.

Seen in this light, Disney's *High School Musical* may not be the nerd-transcended miracle it purports to be. It may, in fact, be the final nail in the coffin of American economic competitiveness, because it is the most popular entertainment ever with tweens, those youngsters who are particularly desperate to figure out what life in high school is really like. They watch the movie, and they get two messages: (1) In the rigid social world of high school, nerds and geeks are at the bottom of the social hierarchy; and (2) If you are miraculously talented in something else, like music, you can get out of your straitjacket. One message is about the norms of high school; the other is a lovely fantasy. Which is the takeaway message for tweens? We don't know for sure, but I'd be willing to make a bet it's not the one about "breakin' free."

HOME REMEDIES

With such a complex, multifaceted, essentially cultural problem, it is easy for parents to feel overwhelmed. But when our kids start showing the ill effects of nerd stereotyping, we can't just throw in the towel. "It's anti-intellectualism, honey . . . that's what America is all about" is not an acceptable parental response, even if it's true. Unfortunately, we can't send a letter of complaint to the national cultural czar and beg him or her to intervene. But we can send a message to more important recipients—our kids—that we will not tolerate cultural stereotypes that impoverish their future lives. Here are a few practical suggestions for belea-guered parents of nerd-bashing kids:

Get specific. For kids who are using the term "nerd" or "geek" in a pejorative manner, we can first try to figure out what they mean. As we have seen, kids often don't mean the same things adults do when they use the stereotypes, so a little investigation is a good place to start. When they describe a classmate as "nerdy," do they mean "too compliant," or "too immersed in fan-tasy," or "too shy"? When we know exactly what they mean, we can intervene in a more enlightened fashion. If nothing else, we let them know that using stereotypes is lazy; being more specific is a better place to start a serious conversation. Of course this means parents have to expunge the words from their own vocab-ularies. Since I began writing this book, I have, in my conversa-tion, forsworn using the adjective "nerdy" just to see if it can be done. And it can. I have found myself thinking more clearly, and specifically, about what I mean, rather than using a handy but ultimately lazy and degrading shorthand.

Stop using nerdity as an excuse. That degradation thing has to go, too. Often parents deride other kids for being nerdy or geeky as compensation for their own kids' failures. If another kid beats yours in a spelling bee or a math quiz or a science fair, it is tempting to make your kid feel better by dumping on the enemy: "Of course he beat you! He's such a nerd—what else does he have to do but study?" As we have noted, vilifying others who are excellent is probably not a good idea; our kids just get the idea that excellence in science or math or school is repugnant. Think of athletic competition as a model: If another kid beats ours in a race, we don't say, "I think it's obnoxious that kid won. Wouldn't you rather be liked and come in second than win and have everybody hate you?" We just wouldn't do it; when it comes to athletics, we always want our kids to get the message that excellence is worth striving for. Why not apply the same thinking to "harrrd" schoolwork?

Find appropriate models. If our kids have the notion that excellence in science or math is social death, we can gently disabuse them of that notion. This is not easy, but we may get some help from the young and hip. For kids who are struggling in math or science in school, I often recommend that parents find a tutor who is a living counterexample. Rather than a retired schoolteacher or engineer, try to find a young, attractive college student of your child's gender to help him or her with math or science. It's hard to assert that math and science are for losers when an obvious winner is coming over to help you out. It doesn't have to be a college math major—any college kid who has taken calculus can tutor a middle or high school student. The tutor need only be admirable, and fashionable.

Turn off the brainwashers. There is no reason to allow kids, at least those in elementary and middle school, to watch television shows or movies that explicitly denigrate intelligence. There's plenty of other stuff to watch. All those forensic scientist shows are just fine: Those hot people in the white coats are, after all, forensic *scientists*. But most shows made for tweens need to be carefully prescreened. And while we're at it, let's stop fooling ourselves about stereotypes transcended; these are just vehicles for viral marketing of negative images of studious kids. We can turn off *Beauty and the Geek* and stop going mad over *High School Musical*, and it's about time we did.

For parents of the nerd-labeled, the recommendations are simple to understand but difficult to carry out. Most of the following boil down to one word: patience. Here are a few suggestions:

Look to the future. Most nerd-labeled kids will eventually be just fine, but they have to wait out middle school and, sometimes, the early years of high school. It is very hard for kids to wait, but that's what they need to do, and knowing that can sometimes make things a little easier. One talented student I know, who accelerated into high school classes during eighth grade, told me: "It's not only that kids in high school are nicer. What's really amazing is that even the kids who were total jerks in middle school are nicer." Kids really do become more tolerant of outliers in high school, and our nerd-labeled kids need to hear that over and over.

Find a subculture. Most parents of the nerd-labeled already do this, but those who don't should start right away. If there are only a few kids in your child's school like him or her, you need to find an activity that includes kids from other schools. Scouting, chess clubs, and especially music lessons or ensembles are great havens for nerd-labeled kids, allowing them to hang out with like-minded kids in a friendly atmosphere until their peers catch up and realize how cool they really are. Summer camps are a great way for kids with unusual passions to meet friends they will keep for life, now that keeping friends in other places is so easy to do. Music lessons are the ultimate revenge of the nerd, as we know. Early on, kids are derided for studying music, for practicing, for being "band nerds." But later, in high school and in college, all those skills, if cultivated and deployed, can turn a lonely music student into the front man or woman for a suddenly popular band, with all the attendant social amenities that affords. A useful motto: "When discouraged, remember Moby."

Compromise with the enemy. This may seem a contradiction to the previous recommendation, but it is important for parents to help their nerd-labeled kids be more popular. This involves plenty of examination about one's own standards and values. If you are an uncompromising parent who believes that "what's important is on the inside," good for you. That is all true. But kids really do need to live through seventh grade. If they want contact lenses, get them. If they want to work on their athletic skills, help them do so. Help them blend in. Fashion may not be all that important, but it is not necessarily a sellout. As we have seen, simple compromises can be made with surprising results. There is a big world of gray between the black of seventh-grade viciousness and the white of totally protective home-schooling. Parents can help their nerd-labeled kids find a middle ground that feels comfortable enough while everyone waits for the situation to improve (see above).

CULTURAL CHANGE
BEGINS AT HOME

Parents can move mountains for their kids, but the mountain that really needs moving is our cultural milieu itself. As we have seen in the pages of this book, nerd/geek stereotypes are a complex amalgam of old and new trends in American thought and social organization. They are the new avatars of very old fantasies, with an overlay that is uniquely American and uniquely twenty-first century. If we wanted to take the low road to sabotage America's economic competitors, we could, of course, work as hard as possible to pollute the whole world with images of scary, repulsive nerds and geeks; pretty soon no kid anywhere will want to study electrical engineering. But if we wanted to be more constructive (as I hope we do), here are a few steps we might take. Most of them are pretty difficult, but we need to begin somewhere.

Keep Ichabod Crane out of school. We could try to remember that the Man of Action–Man of Reflection dichotomy is a historical theme that doesn't really work to our advantage anymore. Therefore, we could teach literature like "The Legend of Sleepy Hollow" in college as an example of big mistakes in American history rather than as a model for American behavior. There's plenty of literature, like Harry Potter and the *Odyssey*, that features heroes who are smart, attractive, courageous, and physically competent, all at the same time. Let's teach those works to kids and save Ichabod Crane and Brom Bones for later.

Make stereotyping shameful. Censorship is awfully difficult, but couldn't we at least try a little shame? Could we remember that when we peddle nerd/geek stereotypes on T-shirts or websites, we are doing something destructive, not something harmlessly funny? People might start to feel embarrassed if they realize they are doing something tasteless if not downright harmful. Talking about nerds and geeks to kids could be like telling them dirty jokes: not really awful but pretty awful and something that calls the judgment of the teller into question. Toy-store owners could stop selling "nerd glasses." Keep them in novelty stores, next to the floaty pens, the ones depicting people whose clothes come off when you tip them over—maybe this is okay. But keep them out of stores where little kids shop for toys. These stereotypes could be redefined, one person at a time, as exemplars of poor taste, especially when used around children.

Do some homework. When I began this book, I fully expected to find a world of social science research on the topic of nerd/geek stereotypes to supplement my own observations of kids and families, but it's not there. Despite the urgency that blue-ribbon scientists and businesspeople feel, no one seems to be particularly interested in rigorously controlled studies of the development of these stereotypes and their effects on kids' self-esteem, achievement, and life choices. Is it because the stereotypes seem inevitable? Attitudes can change, and they can be changed, but first we need to know what we're dealing with. This book is a start, but there's a lot of homework to do, and so far, very few seem to be interested in doing it.

Cut out the lazy characterizations. This one is especially for journalists, who seem to be more and more convinced that brevity is the soul of profit. In such a world, stereotypes like "nerd" and "geek" save time as well as precious column inches. But as we have seen, the terms are so overdetermined that they don't really say anything at all. They just reveal the writer's laziness. So maybe it's time for journalists, or those who purport to care about precision in print, to work a little harder at finding a way to say something, even if it costs a few extra words.

Act your age. It is scary, truly scary, to get old in America now. We all know it, but trying to be hip by acting like a teenager is unbecoming, and it makes you look ridiculous. If you were nerd-labeled in high school, picking on nerdy kids now is not going to help, and if you were a pop in high school and you're still picking on geeky people of any age, it is time for you to grow up. Try a little dignity, which means standing up for inclusive values rather than sneering at people. It's not that hard, and once you get used to it, it can be . . . well, dignified.

Mind your metaphors. This one is the most difficult by far, but we can try to stop and think about the metaphoric language we use when we talk about science and technology. We can try to move beyond the language of "hard" sciences and "soft" sciences; maybe we could even move beyond the terminological dichotomy of science and humanities, as if science were not the most human thing there is. Cold facts, cold logic . . . we can try to listen to ourselves as we talk to our children. If we can't do this, maybe we can at least recover some of the warmth of discovery when we teach science and math. Maybe we can avoid apologizing for math and science and instead convey the passionate human reward attendant on finding just the right answer.

Love our inner salesman a little less. Salesmen and all people who make great eye contact and have smooth social skills are wonderful, but they aren't the exemplars of the human condition. People who seem a little remote or whose eye contact is not so constant are not sick or doomed or crazy; they are just not salesmen. We don't have to vilify shy or awkward people, especially if they are doing a great job at things we know nothing about. We can work harder to respect online life and online communities as real things, even if they are not always fully embodied. And we can be more respectful of and compassionate toward people who are living full lives that don't happen to revolve around the playground or the prom or their adult equivalents.

Love our inner nerds a lot more. Let's all agree once and for all that the Manichean life is not worth living. The world is not made up of healthy, sexy, good pops and jocks and sick, pathetic, bad nerds and geeks. We all have moments, or hours, or years of nerdiness inside us—secret unsocialized passions for things that bore everyone but us; fantasies of being wizards, orcs, or Klingons; wishes to be good Scouts and earn more merit badges; moments of blissful childlike unself-consciousness—it's all in there, in everyone. Hating nerds and geeks is always self-hate, and killing them off in the outside world is just another way of trying to kill them off in the inside. Try to remember that the nerd you save may be yourself.

NOTES

PREFACE TO THE PAPERBACK EDITION

page 3   **I gave an interview to a business reporter:** Steve Lohr, "'Nerd' and 'Geek' Should Be Banned, Professor Says," *The New York Times*, December 21, 2009.

page 4   **In August 2010, a story appeared:** Monica Davey, "A Young Republican with a Sweeping Agenda," *The New York Times*, August 3, 2010.

page 5   **"A bald man with a gray beard":** Michael Grunwald, "The 2009 Person of the Year: Ben Bernanke," *Time*, December 28, 2009/January 4, 2010.

page 6   **(as a recent *New York Times* article about the show points out):** Dennis Overbye, "Exploring the Complexities of Nerdiness for Laughs," *The New York Times*, April 26, 2010.

INTRODUCTION: THE NERD DILEMMA

page 16   **people who wish not to be biased:** S. Christian Wheeler and Richard E. Petty, "The Effects of Stereotype Activation on

Behavior: A Review of Possible Mechanisms," *Psychological Bulletin* 127, no. 6 (2001), 797–826.

1. THE FIELD GUIDE TO NERDS

page 30 **definition of a folk concept:** http://en.wikipedia.org/wiki/Nerd, consulted December 28, 2006.

page 32 **"Pundits and observers":** Ibid.

page 33 **hip young novelist:** Jonathan Lethem, *The Disappointment Artist* (New York: Doubleday, 2005).

page 34 **movies based on comic books:** A. O. Scott, "Summer Movies: Revenge of the Nerds," *The New York Times*, May 8, 2005.

page 35 **The word "nerd" first appeared:** Dr. Seuss, *If I Ran the Zoo* (New York: Random House Books for Young Readers, 1950).

page 35 **In a 1951 *Newsweek* article:** Several websites created by amateur etymologists keep track of, and constantly update, early sightings of the terms "nerd" and "geek." One good example is to be found at http://home.comcast.net/~brons/NerdCorner/nerd.html.

page 37 **"classic" nerd-versus-jock confrontation:** Sarah Vowell, *The Partly Cloudy Patriot* (New York: Simon & Schuster, 2003).

page 38 **brains and physical coordination . . . in the same people:** Lewis Terman and Melita Oden, *The Gifted Group at Mid-Life: Thirty-five Years' Follow-up of the Superior Child* (Stanford, CA: Stanford University Press, 1959).

page 40 **demonstrated . . . by the Gestalt psychologist:** Heinz Werner, *Comparative Psychology of Mental Development* (New York: International Universities Press, 1964).

page 42 **after the Columbine massacre:** Elliot Aronson, *Nobody Left to Hate: Teaching Compassion After Columbine* (New York: W. H. Freeman, 2000).

2. MATH SCORES AND ECONOMIC ILLS

page 56 **science and engineering shortage . . . RAND Corporation study:** William P. Butz, Gabrielle A. Bloom, Mihal E. Gross, Terrence K. Kelly, Aaron Kofner, and Helga E. Rippen, "Is There a Shortage of Scientists and Engineers? How Would We Know?" RAND Corporation Issue Papers, 2003.

page 56 **The 2009 National Science Foundation survey of earned doctorates:** http://www.nsf.gov/statistics/infbrief/nsf10308/.

page 57 **American kids do not measure up:** National Commission on Excellence in Education, *A Nation at Risk: The Imperative for Educational Reform* (Washington, DC: U.S. Government Printing Office, 2003).

page 58 **by 1990 . . . program of educational goals:** National Education Goals Panel, *The National Education Goals Report: Building a Nation of Learners* (Washington, DC: U.S. Government Printing Office, 1996).

page 58 **Program for International Student Assessment:** Organisation for Economic Co-operation and Development, Program for International Student Assessment, 2003. www.pisa.oecd.org.

page 58 **In 2006, the most recent year for which PISA data are available:** http://www.oecd.org/document/2/0,3343,en_32252351_32236191_39718850_1_1_1_1,00.html.

page 58 **Another prestigious achievement survey, the Trends in International Science Study:** http://nces.ed.gov/timss/results07.asp.

page 59 **"Nation's Report Card":** National Center for Education Statistics, National Assessment of Educational Progress. http://nces.ed.gov/nationsreportcard.

page 61 **"math wars":** Leah Vukmir, "2 + 2 = 5: Fuzzy Math Invades Wisconsin Schools," *Wisconsin Interest*, Winter 2001.

page 65 **"Adonis Complex":** Harrison G. Pope, Jr., Katharine Philips, and Roberto Olivardia, *The Adonis Complex: The Secret Crisis of Male Body Obsession* (New York: Free Press, 2000).

page 67   **The one study that comes close:** Klaus Boehnke, Anna-Katharina Pelkner, and Jenny Kurman, "On the Interrelation of Peer Climate and School Performance in Mathematics: A German–Canadian–Israeli Comparison of 14-Year-Old School Students," in B. N. Setiadi et al., eds., *Ongoing Themes in Psychology and Culture* (Selected Papers from the Sixteenth International Congress of the International Association for Cross-Cultural Psychology), 2004. http://www.iaccp.org.

page 68   **One was done in Australia:** Lyn Courtney, Colin Lankshear, Neil Anderson, and Carolyn Timms, "Insider Perspectives vs. Public Perceptions of ICT: Toward Policy for Enhancing Female Student Participation in Academic Pathways to Professional Careers in ICT," *Policy Futures in Education* 7, no. 1 (2009), 44–64.

page 68   **And one study done in England by Heather Mendick:** http://www.sciencedaily.com/releases/2008/05/080512094435.htm.

page 72   **"The nerd/geek stereotype is a luxury":** Mirka Prazak, conversation with the author, September 22, 2006.

page 74   **recent study from . . . Michigan:** See also the survey "Rising to the Challenge: Are High School Graduates Prepared for College and Work?" conducted by Achieve, Inc., February 2005. http://www.achieve.org.

3. OLD THEMES AND NEW TWISTS

page 77   **"He was a native of Connecticut," and quotations following:** Washington Irving, *The Legend of Sleepy Hollow and Other Stories from The Sketch Book* (New York: Signet, 2006).

page 81   **ten most challenged books:** The ALA list is available at its website, http://www.ala.org/ala/oif/bannedbooksweek/bbwlinks/100mostfrequently.htm.

page 83   **the distinct character of the American intellectual:** Kenneth S. Sacks, *Understanding Emerson: "The American Scholar" and His Struggle for Self-Reliance* (Princeton, NJ: Princeton University Press, 2003).

page 84   **"In this distribution of functions," and passages following:** Ralph Waldo Emerson, *Selected Writings of Ralph Waldo Emerson*, ed. William H. Gilman (New York: Signet, 2003).

page 88   **Hofstadter . . . classic work, and discussion following:** Richard Hofstadter, *Anti-intellectualism in American Life* (New York: Vintage, 1966).

pages 90–91   **Superman, the quintessentially American superhero:** Les Daniels, *Superman: The Complete History: The Life and Times of the Man of Steel* (New York: Chronicle, 1998). See also Scott Bukatman, *Matters of Gravity: Special Effects and Supermen in the 20th Century* (Durham, NC: Duke University Press, 2003).

page 93   **really good heroic literature . . . intelligence and physicality and, yes, sexuality:** Homer, *The Odyssey,* trans. Robert Fagles (New York: Penguin, 1996).

page 95   **"The Greeks did not require":** Mary Lefkowitz, e-mail to the author, August 7, 2006.

4. THEY CAN'T HELP IT, THEY'RE JUST SICK

page 99   **"Of course, high-functioning people":** Abigail Sullivan Moore, "A Dream Not Denied: Students on the Spectrum," *The New York Times*, November 5, 2006.

page 101   **mild forms of mental illness:** John J. Ratey and Catherine Johnson, *Shadow Syndromes: The Mild Forms of Major Mental Disorders That Sabotage Us* (New York: Bantam, 1997).

page 101   **"At present the classic":** Ibid.

page 105   ***forme fruste* movement:** Peter D. Kramer, *Listening to Prozac: A Psychiatrist Explores Antidepressant Drugs and the Remaking of the Self* (New York: Viking, 1993).

page 108 **"Specialists say teenagers with Asperger's Syndrome":** Jessica Heslam, "Experts: Teen Years Tough for Asperger's Sufferers," *Boston Herald*, January 20, 2007.

page 109 **the bible of the mental-health business:** *Diagnostic and Statistical Manual of Mental Disorders*, 4th ed. (*DSM-IV*) (Washington, DC: American Psychiatric Association, 1994).

page 110 **diagnostic criteria for Asperger's syndrome:** Ibid.

page 112 **prevalence of AS and autism:** M. F. Blaxill, "What's Going On? The Question of Time Trends in Autism," *Public Health Reports* 119, no. 6 (2004), 536–551.

page 117 **"On *Smallville*, John Schneider":** John Morgan, "John Schneider Promotes Asperger's Syndrome Awareness," USA.com, April 15, 2003.

page 119 **real nineteenth-century mental "illness":** Carol Tavris, "The Illusion of Science in Psychiatry," *Skeptic* 2, no. 3 (1994), 77–85.

page 121 **current hot-button issues:** Steve Silberman, "The Geek Syndrome," *Wired* 9, no. 12 (December 2001).

5. THE SEINFELD AXIOM

page 131 **Why should people . . . evolutionary goal?:** An introduction to some of these questions may be found in Clive Thompson, "Music of the Hemispheres," *The New York Times*, December 31, 2006.

page 132 **position taken by followers of Piaget:** David Elkind, *Child Development and Education* (New York: Oxford University Press, 1976). Elkind's ideas are presented in more popular form in his more recent book *The Hurried Child: Growing Up Too Fast, Too Soon* (New York: Perseus, 2001).

page 134 **a concept like "attractiveness":** Judith H. Langlois, Lisa Kalakanis, Adam J. Rubenstein, Andrea Larson, Monica Hallam, and Monica Smoot, "Maxims or Myths of Beauty? A Meta-analytic and Theoretical Review," *Psychological Bulletin* 126, no. 3 (May 2000), 390–423.

page 137 **romance author . . . has made a career:** Vicki Lewis Thompson, *Nerd in Shining Armor* (New York: Dell, 2003); *Nerd Gone Wild* (New York: St. Martin's, 2005); *The Nerd Who Loved Me* (New York: St. Martin's, 2006). There are many others in this series, with no apparent end in sight.

page 138 **smart kids . . . In 2000, a study titled:** Carolyn Tucker Halpern, Kara Joyner, J. Richard Udry, and Chirayath Suchindran, "Smart Teens Don't Have Sex (or Kiss Much, Either)," *Journal of Adolescent Health* 26, no. 3 (March 2000), 213–225.

page 144 **late sexual initiation . . . religiosity:** Jennifer S. Manlove, Elizabeth Terry-Humen, Erum Ikramullah, and Kristin Moore, "The Role of Parent Religiosity in Teens' Transitions to Sex and Contraception," *Journal of Adolescent Health* 39 no. 4 (October 2006), 578–587.

page 145 **Kids who have more parental inputs:** A recent example of this kind of research can be found in William Fowler, Karen Ogston, Gloria Roberts, and Amy Swenson, "The Effects of Early Language Enrichment," *Early Child Development and Care* 176, no. 8 (December 2006), 777–815. The "confluence model," which explains IQ differences based on parental inputs, has been developed and researched over many years by Robert Zajonc. See, for example, Robert Zajonc and Patricia Mullaly, "Birth Order: Reconciling Conflicting Effects," *American Psychologist* 52, no. 7 (July 1997), 685–699.

page 146 **teen brain . . . in the news:** Shannon Brownlee and Roberta Hotinski, "Inside the Teen Brain," *U.S. News & World Report,* August 9, 1999.

page 148 **some lower mammals, sex . . . stupid:** S. Marc Breedlove, "Sex on the Brain," *Nature* 389 (1997), 801.

page 149 **experiments with . . . monogamous prairie voles:** Larry J. Young and Zuoxin Wang, "The Neurobiology of Pair Bonding," *Nature Neuroscience* 10, no. 7 (October 2004), 1048–1054.

page 150 **Normal humans show . . . prolactin:** S. Brody and T. H. Kruger, "The Post-Orgasmic Prolactin Increase Following Intercourse Is Greater than Following Masturbation and Suggests Greater Satiety," *Biological Psychology* 71, no. 3 (March 2006), 312–315.

6. THE GEEK SQUAD

page 162 **NASA's turning to tinkerers:** Jack Hitt, "The Amateur Future of Space Travel," *The New York Times Magazine*, July 1, 2007.

page 162 **best inventions for the year 2006:** Lev Grossman, "Best Inventions 2006," *Time,* November 13, 2006.

page 173 **Metaphorical entailments made their debut:** George S. Lakoff and Mark Johnson, *Metaphors We Live By* (Chicago: University of Chicago Press, 1980).

page 174 **interface between literature and psychology:** Burton Melnick, "Cold Hard World \ Warm Soft Mommy: The Unconscious Logic of Metaphor," *The Annual of Psychoanalysis* 28 (2000), 225–244.

7. THEY'RE NOT UGLY,
THEY JUST NEED A MAKEOVER

page 184 **market forces unleashed by the tween phenomenon:** Alicia de Mesa, "Marketing and Tweens," *BusinessWeek,* October 12, 2005. Also see "Marketing to Tweens Going Too Far?" CBS News, May 14, 2007. http://www.cbsnews.com/stories/2007/05/14/earlyshow/living/parenting/main2.

page 185 **how much identity formation has changed:** Erik Erikson, *Childhood and Society* (New York: W. W. Norton, 1950).

page 187 **"It's hard to write this":** Lawrence Downes, "Middle School Girls Gone Wild," *The New York Times,* December 29, 2006.

page 189 **identity consolidation:** Gil Noam, "The Psychology of Belonging," in A. H. Esman and L. T. Flaherty, eds., *Adolescent Psychiatry: Developmental and Clinical Processes* (Hillsdale, NJ: Analytic Press, 1999).

page 193 **"Hey scoutdad":**http://forums.freep.com/viewtopic.php?t=8702&view=next&sid=4a24fc279eecbdc33716b5b8085df369.

page 194 **"[The new dollar coins] feature a different president":** Joel Stein, "The Buck Stops Here: Presidential Coins Aren't Enough to Wean Americans off the Dopey Dollar Bill," *Los Angeles Times*, February 20, 2007.

8. I'M NOT BORING YOU, AM I?

page 223 **study looking at the fantasy lives of our subjects:** David Anderegg, "Predicting Children's Sociometric Status from Their Fantasy Self-Representations." Unpublished dissertation, Clark University, Worcester, MA, 1985.

9. WELCOME TO MY PERSECUTION

page 227 **"Gore's pencil neck tugs," and quotations following:** Vowell, *The Partly Cloudy Patriot.*

page 231 **Jung's description of archetypes:** Carl Jung, *The Archetypes and The Collective Unconscious*, vol. 9, part 1, of *Collected Works*, 2nd ed. (Princeton, NJ: Bollingen, 1981).

page 233 **The always irksome Joel Stein:** Joel Stein, "The Jokes Are on Obama," *Los Angeles Times*, July 18, 2008.

page 240 **The nickname thing:** James E. Mueller, *Towel Snapping the Press: Bush's Journey from Locker-Room Antics to Message Control* (Lanham, MD: Rowman & Littlefield, 2006).

page 241 **the W presidency did not turn out:** Paul Krugman, "All the President's Enablers," *The New York Times*, July 20, 2007.

page 243 **The Delta Zeta massacre:** Sam Dillon, "Evictions at Sorority Raise Issue of Bias," *The New York Times*, February 25, 2007.

page 244 **The Asian pop-music blackball:** Mireya Navarro, "Trying to Crack the Hot 100," *The New York Times*, March 4, 2007.

page 244 **The likable-president recurring nightmare:** David Brooks, "Neither Clinton, nor Obama," *The New York Times*, March 4, 2007.

CONCLUSION: THE NERD YOU SAVE

page 254 **final report from the Committee on Science, Engineering, and Public Policy:** Committee on Science, Engineering, and Public Policy, *Rising Above the Gathering Storm: Energizing and Employing America for a Brighter Economic Future* (Washington, DC: National Academics Press, 2005).

page 256 **Many college anti–binge-drinking campaigns:** David Hines, Renee Saris, and Leslee Throckmorton-Belzer, "Pluralistic Ignorance and Health Risk Behaviors: Do College Students Misperceive Social Approval for Risky Behaviors on Campus and in Media?" *Journal of Applied Social Psychology* 32, no. 12 (December 2002), 2621–2640.

INDEX

INDEX

INDEX

If you enjoyed this book, visit

www.tarcherbooks.com

and sign up for Tarcher's e-newsletter to receive
special offers, giveaway promotions, and
information on hot upcoming releases.

TARCHER
PENGUIN

Great Lives Begin with Great Ideas

If you would like to place a bulk order
of this book, call 1-800-847-5515.